Arthur Lyman Tuckerman

A Short History of Architecture

Arthur Lyman Tuckerman

A Short History of Architecture

ISBN/EAN: 9783337321994

Printed in Europe, USA, Canada, Australia, Japan

Cover: Foto ©ninafisch / pixelio.de

More available books at **www.hansebooks.com**

A SHORT HISTORY

OF

ARCHITECTURE

BY

ARTHUR LYMAN TUCKERMAN

WITH ILLUSTRATIONS BY THE AUTHOR

NEW YORK

CHARLES SCRIBNER'S SONS

1887

"To build, to build!
That is the noblest art of all the arts.
Painting and Sculpture are but images,
Are merely shadows cast by outward things
On stone or canvas, having in themselves
No separate existence. Architecture,
Existing in itself, and not in seeming
A something it is not, surpasses them
As substance shadow."
—LONGFELLOW, in *Michael Angelo.*

PREFACE.

I HAVE written this short history of architecture to meet the requirements of those who wish to become acquainted with the main facts without having to read voluminous works, many of which are addressed, not to the student, but to the connoisseur, who is presumed at the start to have a knowledge of the subject sufficient to enable him to comprehend critical and theoretical essays.

The plan I have adopted has been to trace the origin of each style, its characteristic points and its connection with those which preceded and succeeded it, without introducing technical terms or any but the most important dates.

There is a temptation to enter into the social and political histories of each building race, but brevity forbids this, as well as any of the gushing descriptions usually found in modern handbooks on art.

I imagine that very few people have the time to read lengthy treatises on architecture, but that there are many who would be glad to know the chief historical facts, were these to be presented within a small compass. I hope, therefore, that this volume may be of interest to the general reader and may find its way to schools other than those which make art matters their specialty, for it seems to me that if the average schoolboy were taught as much about the history of the most useful and beautiful of the creations of the people of each age, as about the manner and quantity of warfare and slaughter in which they indulged, he would obtain as valuable a quality of information.

 Art Schools of the Metropolitan Museum,
   March, 1887

LIST OF PLATES.

St. Trophyme at Arles,	*Frontispiece.*
	FACING PAGE
The Greek Orders,	56
Plan of the Temple of Theseus at Athens,	62
The Roman Orders,	70
Palace of Diocletian at Spalatro,	73
Plan of the Pantheon at Rome,	74
Plan of the Baths of Agrippa,	75
Plan of the Temple of the Sun at Baalbek,	76
Plan of the Old Basilica of St. Paul's Beyond the Walls,	89
St. Vitale, of Ravenna,	92
The Temple of Minerva Medica,	93
The Temple of Vesta, sometimes called the Temple of Hercules,	94

LIST OF PLATES.

	FACING PAGE
THE BAPTISTERY OF CONSTANTINE,	94
THE PENDENTIVE SYSTEM IN BYZANTINE DOMES,	97
CHURCH OF SERGIUS AND BACCHUS AT CONSTANTINOPLE,	98
PLAN OF ST. SOPHIA, CONSTANTINOPLE,	99
ROMANESQUE CONSTRUCTION,	121
COMPARATIVE SERIES, SHOWING GREEK, ROMAN, ROMANESQUE, AND GOTHIC METHODS OF SUPPORT,	124
PLAN OF STRASBOURG CATHEDRAL,	128
CHEVET OF NOTRE DAME DU PORT AT CLERMONT,	130
PLAN OF RHEIMS CATHEDRAL,	134
PLAN OF AN ENGLISH CATHEDRAL,	136
PLAN OF ST. PETER'S AS ORIGINALLY DESIGNED BY MICHAEL ANGELO,	155
PLAN OF CHURCH OF THE HOTEL DES INVALIDES AT PARIS,	160

CONTENTS.

	PAGE
INTRODUCTION,	1
I.—CELTIC OR DRUIDICAL REMAINS,	5
II.—THE MONUMENTS OF EGYPT,	10
III.—ASIATIC ARCHITECTURE,	30
IV.—GREECE,	52
V.—ETRURIA AND ROME,	68
VI.—THE EARLY CHRISTIAN STYLE,	88
VII.—THE BYZANTINE STYLE,	95
VIII.—MAHOMETAN ARCHITECTURE,	105
IX.—THE ROMANESQUE STYLE,	115
X.—GOTHIC ARCHITECTURE,	132
XI.—THE RENAISSANCE,	151
XII.—CONCLUSION,	162

A SHORT
HISTORY OF ARCHITECTURE.

INTRODUCTION.

ARCHITECTURE is an art combining the qualities of utility and beauty. Its object is, and has been from its origin, to satisfy both the necessities and tastes of the various building races.

For this purpose the two distinct, and yet closely related, sciences of construction and decoration have been employed, and the history of the progress which has been made in each, goes hand in hand with the history of each age and each race.

The requirements of the inhabitants of every country have always been defined by its character and climate, and, in order to satisfy these requirements, the art has adapted itself to them and grown up and expanded in the different fields in which it has been directed.

It is customary to explain the origin of the art of building somewhat as follows: The first impulse of the barbarian, in whatever part of the globe he may be born, is to seek a shelter from the varying temperature of night and day. If he lives in the mountains, he chooses the caves and clefts in the rocks for his habitation; if on the plain, he follows the example of the animals and hollows out a retreat in the ground where he may seek warmth and protection. Where the soil is rocky, he gathers branches and moss, and piles them in such a manner as to form a rude dwelling. Soon after, he perceives the inconvenience of these untrimmed boughs, and remedies the discomfort by driving four straight posts into the ground, and roofing them over with cross-pieces, inclined so as to shed the rain.

This is the first semblance of a thoughtful construction, and the improvements upon it gradually develop into the more studied forms of architecture.

When the first requisite of shelter has been obtained, the early builder cuts off the rough edges and carves upon the posts rude emblems of the natural objects he sees about him, and in doing this takes the first step in design and decoration.

When wood is not abundant, he seeks a similar result in stone, and the treatment of each material gives rise to distinct principles of construction.

The Greeks, who had marble-quarries of easy access, bridged over their posts or columns with straight lintels, capable of supporting the weight of the roof without danger of fracture. The Romans, who found their travertine difficult to handle, built their baths and palaces of brick, and, in seeking to connect their pillars and piers, adopted the round arch as a means of effecting this end, and this round arch was the main principle of Roman architecture. When, in due time, the pointed arch was found to combine great strength and beauty, this new method of building became the leading principle of Gothic art. So, according to each necessity, the different styles of architecture arose.

When civilization increases the requirements of man, it is no longer possible to begin a rude construction, and alter it afterward to suit these needs; therefore it becomes necessary to consider beforehand all the elements required, and, in order to facilitate this consideration, drawing comes in as a simple means of placing before one all that enters into the proposed building.

Therefore, in the study of architecture four divisions of the art must be considered, namely : The construction of buildings with various materials, the appropriate proportions of the same, their representation by draughtsmanship and their history in various times and among various peoples.

It will be readily understood that each of these divisions embraces a wide scope individually, and yet no one can be separated from the others without affecting the result as a whole.

It is proposed, therefore, to review briefly the history of this art, and the causes which have affected it, in order that, knowing the reasons which led to the formation of each style, the student may follow its study with the practical understanding and logical inference which lead to the best results.

The question of which country furnished the first or earliest period of approach to civilization in the building of monuments or habitations has been, and is likely to be, an open one for some time to come.

Speculative discussion on this point can serve no end of importance to architects; it interests more especially the historian and antiquarian. Consequently we will, for the sake of convenience, glance over the periods of architecture in the following order:

1. Celtic or Druidical remains.
2. The Monuments of Egypt.
3. Asiatic architecture.
4. Greece.
5. Etruria and Rome.
6. The Early Christian style.
7. The Byzantine style.
8. Mahometan architecture.
9. The Romanesque style.
10. Gothic architecture.
11. The Renaissance.

I.

CELTIC OR DRUIDICAL REMAINS.

THE Celtic race has left enduring marks of its power in the numerous monuments which are found in various parts of Great Britain, France, Germany, and Spain, and scattered through adjacent countries.

These consist of collections of huge uncarved boulders, arranged in geometrical lines, and often found in the centre of vast plains, far removed from quarry or mountain-side.

The more common forms are called "menhirs or peulvans," signifying in Celtic "long stones." These are either found separately or ranged in long parallel lines.

The most remarkable examples are at Carnac, in Brittany, where there are twelve hundred of these huge stones, varying from three to eighteen feet in height, ranged in eleven rows, leading to a semicircular enclosure.

What purpose they served, and whether of a religious or civil character, has not been conclusively determined. Some consider that they served to mark the burial-spot of the Druids; others that they were landmarks or emblems of victory.

To another class belong the so-called Rocking Stones, which consist of two immense blocks of rock, placed one upon the other, and either balanced so exactly that the slightest touch will suffice to shake them, or pivoted so as to revolve. There are examples at Tenanville, near Cherbourg, in the north of France, and in Sussex, England. One of these, called the "Great upon Little," is estimated to weigh a million pounds.

Batissier considers them to have been erected by the priests, either to strike terror and wonder into the hearts of the people, whom they sought to hold in subjection, or as emblems of the world suspended in the air. We know that they have existed from remote ages, as mention is made of their antiquity by Pliny and Ptolemy.

Trilitha, or lichavens, are formed with three stones, two vertical and one horizontal resting upon the others, in the shape of a rude gateway. This is what they were probably intended for, though it has been suggested that they were used for altars. Similar to these are the dolmens, or table-stones, consisting of one large flat boulder supported by several smaller ones. Their upper surfaces, as a rule, have channels cut in them, which are generally believed to have been receptacles for the blood of victims sacrificed upon them, and some are even hollowed out in the shape of the human body.

The Merchants' Tables, at Lochmariaker, are the most noted among the many that still exist.

From fragments of skeletons usually found in the vicinity of dolmens, it has been imagined that either the priests or their human offerings were buried there as upon consecrated ground.

There are several instances where these dolmens form covered ways or avenues, being placed one beside another in continuous line, and generally surrounded by a plantation of trees. They are frequently divided by blocks of stone into several compartments, and, like the tumuli or barrows, were probably used as places of interment for the dead.

The most interesting, perhaps, of any of these groups of stones are the "cromlechs": enclosures formed of numerous boulders, arranged either in elliptic rows or in concentric circles, with a large monolith in the central point. Each circle is composed of a definite number of "menhirs," and the whole is usually surrounded by a ditch.

It is supposed that each stone represented a minor deity, and the central one the chief of the gods. Their purpose apparently was to mark the place of large assemblies, called together for the administration of civil, military, and religious rites.

The cromlech of Stonehenge in Wiltshire is the most celebrated and one of the largest known. The country folk call it the Cor-Gaur, or dance of giants, and attribute its formation to the magic of the famous enchanter, Merlin. It is composed of two circular and two elliptic enclosures, the one within the other, and is several hundred feet in circumference.

In none of these Celtic monuments is there anything which may be called strictly architectural, but some of them illustrate a principle of building which is of importance to note. To place a row of stones in upright positions denotes no special phase of intelligent thought, beyond a desire to permanently mark some interesting locality, but when the ancient race which raised these massive rocks conceived the idea of supporting one block upon a number of smaller ones, it had reached a first principle of construction, destined to be employed for many centuries afterward in some of the finest buildings. After the trilithon came the table-stones, and from these it was but a step to the covered alleys, which were in themselves a first conception of a rude habitation, walled in and roofed over. There can be nothing more elementary than this, and no simpler constructional expedient, in whatever country it may first have been evolved. We do not know the precise date of Celtic monuments, nor is it probable that they are as ancient as the Egyptian pyramids, but as in any case they illustrate the transition from brutal ignorance to an era of thought, we may place them at the commencement of our chronological list.

In the various themes and discussions advanced by archæologists, and the strange legends and tales of the peasantry with regard to them, we have no concern. It is sufficient for us to know that they exist and afford us an insight into the dawning efforts of a barbaric people to progress in the art which we propose to study.

II.

THE MONUMENTS OF EGYPT.

THE history of Egypt is divided into five periods, from the earliest ages down to its conquest by the Romans at the beginning of the Christian era. The first period comprises the first fourteen dynasties of ancient kings, among whom the most important are : Menes, founder of Memphis, Shoofoo or Cheops, Shafra or Chephren, and Mycerinus, builders of the pyramids of Gizeh, and the two Theban monarchs, Osirtasen I. and Amenemha III., by whom the tombs at Beni Hassan, the Labyrinth and Lake Moeris were constructed. According to Bunsen these fourteen dynasties date from 3623 to 2547 B.C.

The second period is marked by the invasion of the Hyksos, or Shepherd Kings, of whom there were three dynasties. They remained in power until 1625 B.C. and were a warlike and destructive race, leaving no permanent traces of their occupation.

The third period is the most brilliant in Egyptian history, extending from 1625 to 525 B.C., and comprising nine dynasties of great conquerors and builders. The best known of these are : Amosis, Thothmes III., Sethi I., Rameses II. (the Great), called also Sesostris, and Rameses III. Under these kings the great temples of Luxor, Abydus, and Karnak were erected and the arts were assiduously cultivated.

The Persians under Cambyses occupied the country in the year 525 B.C. They were expelled a century later, but were again victorious in 340 B.C., and remained in possession until the conquest of Alexander the Great in 332. This fourth period was as unproductive in works of art as had been that of the Hyksos' dominion.

After Alexander, the Ptolemys ruled until the close of the first century before Christ. Their government promoted the cultivation of the arts and industries and formed the fifth and last period in the history of ancient Egypt as an independent state.

Of these five epochs there are, therefore, only three —namely, the first, third, and fifth—during which architecture flourished, and these three in reality form but one long period in the history of an art which remained almost unaltered, scarcely either improving or receding, from the remotest times to its last day.

Our knowledge of ancient Egypt has been chiefly derived from bass-reliefs, mural paintings and hieroglyphics. The latter were unintelligible until the discovery of the Rosetta stone by the French consul Champollion, in 1798. This was part of a stone tablet bearing three inscriptions, one in hieroglyphics, one in the Cursive letters used by the lower classes, and the third in Greek. By means of this the old alphabet was reconstructed and all the ancient inscriptions deciphered.

TOMBS.

The most important monuments of the first period are the pyramids, the oldest of which were built between three and four thousand years before Christ.

There remain about a hundred of these in the vicinity of the ancient city of Memphis, extending over a considerable extent of country, and others are found in Thebes and at Meroë in Ethiopia. There have been many theories advanced upon the subject of their origin and purpose, and many arguments set forth seeking to prove that they were observatories, temples, granaries, meteorological monuments, or tombs. Nearly all modern authorities agree upon the last as the most probable solution of the problem, not only from the sarcophagi and mummies found within many of them, and from inscriptions relating events in the lives of important personages which adorn the walls of some of their inner chambers, but from the fact that these buildings are never found beyond the confines of cemeteries.

In erecting these monuments, the Egyptians usually selected a site upon a rocky plateau, on which a space equal to the superficial area required for the base was made level, a mound being left in the centre which was bonded in with the masonry. Below this platform a sepulchral chamber and connecting passage were hollowed in the rock. The pyramid was built over this chamber and contained one or more additional apartments, reached from the outside by narrow and inclined corridors. It was generally constructed with blocks of limestone, in successive steps receding at an angle varying from forty-five to seventy degrees. The outside was afterward cased with slabs of polished syenite, upon which inscriptions were engraved or painted. The interior chambers and corridors were likewise lined with polished granite, sometimes so mathematically jointed that a needle could not be pushed between the stones. Ceilings were formed by inclined slabs resting against each other or the walls were corbelled inward until they met.

The entrances to the passages were invariably closed and concealed, and portcullises of heavy granite blocks, sliding in grooves, were placed at intervals along the corridors, the more effectually to preserve the sepulchre from violation. Nearly all have, nevertheless, been entered and rifled, so that but little is left to aid the archæologist in his researches. Fragmentary inscriptions and local observations compared with the accounts given by Greek and Latin authors have, however, resulted in the piecing together of what may be presumed to be an accurate history of the pyramid-builders.

The three largest pyramids are situated at Gizeh, a small village near Cairo, and are respectively those of Cheops, known also as Suphis or Shoofoo, Chephren or Shafra, and Mycerinus.

The following table shows the dimensions given by two of the best authorities:

	Side of Base.		Perpendicular Height.	
	Sir G. Wilkinson.	Col. H. Vyse.	Sir G. Wilkinson.	Col. H. Vyse.
Cheops	756'	764'	480' 9''	480' 9''
Chephren		707' 9''	453'	454' 3''
Mycerinus		364' 6''		208'

All of these are oriented and the entrances are all on the North sides. This is a rule applicable to all the pyramids except that of Sakkarah, which is placed without reference to the points of the compass and was probably erected at a much later date.

The first or Great Pyramid contains one subterranean chamber, reached by a passage some three hundred feet long, and two other apartments above the level of the ground, the one above the other, called the King's and Queen's sepulchres. The entrance to the connecting corridors is placed 45 feet above the ground and 23 feet away from the true centre in order to deceive explorers. The Queen's Chamber is about 18 feet square by 20 feet in height, and is placed directly under the apex of the pyramid. It is 67 feet above the ground, and 71 feet below the King's Chamber. The passage leading to the latter is 28 feet high, formed by corbelled walls. This chamber is roofed by a flat ceiling and measures 34 feet in length by 17 in breadth, and is 19 feet high. The walls and ceiling are built of finely polished granite, and the apartment contains a sarcophagus of the same material. The weight of the superincumbent masonry is relieved by five other compartments placed over the chamber, four of which are covered by flat slabs, and the fifth by inclined stones resting against each other. It was in this highest compartment that some hieroglyphics scrawled in red ochre on the walls were discovered, by means of which the name Shoofoo became known. Herodotus says that one hundred thousand men were employed during twenty years in building the Great Pyramid, after they had devoted ten years, previous to its erection, to the construction of a causeway to the Nile, over which the stone was carried, which had been brought down the river from the Arabian hills.

Diodorus asserts that the number of workmen employed was upward of three hundred and sixty thousand.

The second pyramid contains two chambers, the most important of which is on the ground level, partly sunk in the rock. Its dimensions are 46 feet long by 16 in width, and 22 feet high. Within it a granite sarcophagus was found, containing the bones of an ox. This discovery gave rise to much speculation, as to whether the pyramids were not originally intended for the sepulchres of the animal deities worshipped by the Egyptians, the bull Apis in particular. The third pyramid was covered by a casing of polished red granite, formed of blocks with bevelled edges. There are several chambers inside, one of which contained a mummy and case, now transferred to the British Museum.

Near the pyramid of Cheops, on the same plateau, is the Sphinx. This great statue, with a human head and the body of a lion, is carved in the natural rock, deficiencies being made up by added masonry. Its dimensions are colossal, the body being 140 feet long, and the face 30 feet high by 14 feet in breadth. This mysterious creation was intended as the representation of a god, and as such had sacrifices offered before it, as the altars and temples erected beneath it attest. From inscriptions upon a stone found near by, it is known that the Sphinx was called Hor-em-khoo, " The Sun in his Resting-place." The head was originally surmounted by a royal helmet, the face had a beard, fragments of which have been unearthed, and it is otherwise badly mutilated. This 'fanciful creature has doubtless much affinity with the winged bulls and lions of the Assyrian epoch.

The Egyptians also buried their dead in smaller tombs, in subterranean vaults, and in catacombs excavated in the rock of mountainous regions. A great number of these smaller tombs were built in the vicinity of ancient Memphis and are now commonly called "mastabahs." In arrangement they were nearly all similar, the sepulchre consisting of three parts: a temple overground, a pit or well, and a subterranean chamber. The temple was in the shape of a frustum of a pyramid, the walls inclining inward at an angle of seventy degrees. It contained one or several apartments, used as places of assembly for the relatives and friends of the deceased, who came at stated intervals to hold services and to bring offerings of a suitable character. A list of these occasions was placed over the entrance, and on a second tablet or stella, inside, the name, titles, and virtues of the dead were recorded. The walls were brilliantly painted, domestic and religious scenes being the usual subjects depicted. The well-opening was usually concealed and filled with masonry. Its sides were formed of slabs of granite down to rock level and then excavated in the rock, sometimes thirty or forty yards below the surface. From the bottom of the pit a doorway, usually walled up, opened into a chamber containing a stone sarcophagus, in which the mummy was placed.

The finest excavated grottos are found at Beni Hassan and in the neighborhood of Thebes. Those at Beni Hassan follow the type of the "mastabah," having the assembly hall, the well, and the chamber beneath, all being hollowed out of the rock. The sides are decorated with columns, architraves, and cornices, in imitation of constructive architecture, and the ceilings are cut out to represent vaults, the uncarved surfaces being adorned with paintings and hieroglyphics. The columns are especially interesting, as having evidently furnished the Greeks with the model for their Doric temples, and the order has in consequence been called the proto-doric. They have a diameter of five feet and are sixteen feet high; the shaft has sixteen sides with flutings and is surmounted by a tile or abacus. Besides these, there are other columns with capitals in the form of a lotus or papyrus bud, which are more commonly found in Egyptian temples.

The tombs of the kings at Thebes are arranged on a different principle; they consist of long sloping corridors opening into chambers and halls, and penetrating in a continuous line into the mountain rock. There are several groups, the most important of which is situated in the valley of Biban-el-Molook, or the "Gates of the Kings." The tomb of Sethi I., the father of Rameses II., discovered by the explorer Belzoni in the earlier part of the century, is the finest example, the sculpture and paintings which it contains being very remarkable for their execution and of great historical interest, as they illustrate very completely the manners and customs of the ancient Egyptians. Every effort had evidently been made to conceal the tomb, for not only was the entrance closed and covered with loose rock, but the first chamber, reached by a succession of passages and steep staircases, had been walled up and the four sides painted, so as to have the appearance of being the limit of the extent of the tomb. The hollow sound, caused by hammering on the walls at one point, led the explorer to continue his efforts, which were rewarded by the discovery of several more halls and chambers, terminating in a great vaulted chamber, thirty feet long, containing an alabaster sarcophagus. It has been conjectured that many of these excavated grottos were occupied as residences by the kings and great personages of the empire during their lifetime, and converted into sepulchres after death. The custom of relatives meeting at intervals in an assembly hall connected with the tomb does not seem to have prevailed here as at Memphis, but it is not improbable that the great Theban temples were used, if indeed they were not erected for this purpose.

The great mass of the people were not honoured by such magnificent tombs, but were buried in subterranean vaults in the necropolis (Greek, " city of the dead ") attached to each great town. The largest are those of Saïs, Sakkarah near Memphis, Thebes, and Abydus. These underground galleries were reached by deep wells, and often contained several stories of small chambers in which the embalmed bodies were placed, together with vases, statuettes, and other votive offerings. There were also cemeteries in which the animals worshipped by the Egyptians were buried, containing thousands of embalmed birds and reptiles, particularly the ibis and crocodile. The Apis mausoleum at Sakkarah, where the sacred bulls were interred, is one of the most important, the chambers and galleries being excavated in the rock and covering an immense area. The mausoleum was connected with the Serapeum, a temple above ground, where the living bull was worshipped as a deity.

TEMPLES.

There are two classes of Egyptian temples—those hollowed out of the mountain rock, commonly called speos, and those built upon the open plain and distinguished by the term "hypæthral" (Greek, "under air"). The most important of the latter are the temples of Sethi I., at Abydus; Amun re, at Kooneh; the great and small temples of Medeenet Haboo, erected by Rameses III. and Thothmes II.; the Rameseum or Memnonium, of Rameses II.; Luxor and Karnak, at Thebes; and the temples of Denderah, Edfou, and Philæ, built by the Ptolemys. All of these are similar in general plan, consisting of a greater or less number of courts, halls, and sanctuaries, which in each case are placed "en suite," that is, one opening into the other in a continuous line, the larger apartments being in about the centre of this line and gradually diminishing in size, the last chamber being the smallest. As the main characteristics of the largest temples apply in a modified form to the smallest, a description of a complete temple would seem to be the best way of explaining the usual arrangements.

A wall of crude brick usually enclosed the whole structure, which was surrounded by a sacred grove, or tenemos. This wall was entered by an outer gate, or pylon, built in the shape of a frustum of a pyramid, and surmounted by a coved cornice, the doorway having perpendicular or slanting jambs. From this an avenue, or dromos, bordered with sphinxes with human or rams' heads, led up to the propylæa, or towers. The latter resembled the outer pylons, but were on a larger scale, containing staircases leading to upper terraces. They were spaced a short distance apart to admit of a passage between them, which was entered through a second gateway similar to the first. The sides of these buildings were usually elaborately painted, and rings were inserted in the masonry to hold the poles upon which the royal banners were hoisted. This second entrance was often flanked by two obelisks—long tapering monoliths with pyramidal summits, covered with hieroglyphic inscriptions recounting the dedication of the temple by the king to his favorite divinity. These obelisks were sometimes ninety feet high, and mounted upon square blocks. They were not always of equal size, probably owing to the difficulty of obtaining single stones of such enormous length. It is of interest to note that their sides were made slightly convex in order to prevent their appearing concave, which would be the effect had they been left quite flat. A second set of towers, or propylæa, with staircases, came next, with a court or area intervening. On each side of this court a colonnade was generally placed; and sometimes before the entrance to the towers two colossal statues of the king, represented seated, with his hands resting upon his knees in the conventional attitude of repose. The most famous are those known as the Colossi of Memnon, which stand on the plain of Thebes. They were probably in the court of the temple of Amunoph III., of which scarcely any vestige now remains. They are fifty feet high, mounted upon pedestals. One of them is called the Vocal Memnon, as, in ancient times, it gave forth sounds at the break of day—a phenomenon more easily explained as a trick of the priests, than by natural causes.

Beyond this court there was usually an inner vestibule, with columns forming porticos on the four sides; those opposite the entrance being connected by stone screens, reaching half-way up, forming a shaded anteroom, or pronaos, to the great hall of assembly, which was the next apartment.

The shafts and capitals of the columns varied in different buildings. The plain cylinder, carrying an inverted bell decorated with palm or other smaller leaves, or a capital in the shape of the lotus flower were the commonest forms. A column, representing the stems of water-plants bound together with rings, and swelling out at the top in the place of the capital, was also often employed. Besides these, statues of kings, or shafts surmounted by the heads of Isis or Osiris, were used as supports. The architrave, or beam, did not rest directly upon the capital, but upon an intermediate block. This block, when on the heads of deities, was in the shape of a miniature pylon. The cornices were formed of a deep cove and fillet decorated with winged asps.

Some idea of the size of these inner vestibules, or peristyles, may be formed from the dimensions of that in the great temple of Medeenet Haboo, which measures 123 by 133 feet, and has a height of 39 feet 4 inches. Each of the porticos of the East and West sides is supported by five columns; those on the North and South by eight Osiride pillars, having a circumference of 23 feet and a height of 24 feet.

The great hall of assembly, which adjoined the vestibule, was generally the finest portion of the temple. The architraves supporting the roof rested upon a great number of lofty columns, which in the centre rose to a greater height, in order to obtain a clerestory, by which the hall was lighted. The largest of these is in the temple of Karnak, measuring 170 by 329 feet. The central avenue consists of twelve columns, 62 feet high by 11 feet 6 inches in diameter. Besides these there are one hundred and twenty-two others, 42 feet 6 inches in height and 28 feet in circumference. The lintel over the doorway by which it is entered measured 40 feet in length. The sanctuary was contiguous to the great hall, and terminated the suite. This consisted of a chamber, either occupying the whole of the rear space, or isolated by corridors on each side, with smaller sanctuaries opposite. In many of these, altars and statues have been found, some of the former formed of a single block, hollowed at the top and pierced through from top to bottom, so that sacrifices placed upon them could be consumed apparently without ignition, by means of fires kindled in subterranean vaults.

In connection with the halls in the temple of Abydus and elsewhere there were a number of vaulted chambers; the vault not being formed of a series of true arches, that is, with joints radiating to a common centre, but consisting of stone beams placed one beside the other, and hollowed out on the under side. The arch, however, was not unknown to the Egyptians—there are stone vaulted tombs at Sakkarah of the time of Psammetichus (650 B.C.), and crude brick arches have been found at Thebes dating as far back as the period of the eighth dynasty (2925 B.C.?). The antiquity of the arch has been the subject of much debate, owing chiefly to the fact that the Greeks made no use of it; recent explorations have, however, shown that this constructive expedient was known both in Egypt and Assyria many years before it was adopted by the Etruscans, to whom its invention was long attributed.

The exterior walls of all temples were built on a batter, sloping inward at an angle of about seventy degrees and with scarcely any openings. The inside walls were perpendicular, and decorated with bass-reliefs and paintings. These were often of a most elaborate character, and it is from them that so much has been learned concerning the ancient history of the country.

The rock-cut temples of Nubia are laid out on much the same plan. They usually consist of a pronaos, naos, and sanctuary, forming a suite, with an entrance marked by colossal statuary hewn out of the side of the cliff. Some have a dromos of sphinxes, propylæa, and a peristyle court of masonry preceding the excavated portions. The temple of Wady Sabooah is the best example of the latter. Of the former none can compare with the Great and Small temples of Aboo Simbel, or Ipsambool, which are of the time of Rameses the Great.

The smaller of the two is dedicated to the goddess Athor, the Venus of the Egyptians. The exterior is ornamented with six statues of deities recessed in the rock, each measuring thirty-five feet in height. In the interior there is a first hall, supported by square pillars, opening into a corridor, flanked by smaller halls, leading to the sanctuary.

The front of the Great temple is adorned with four statues of the king seated upon his throne, each sixty feet high. In the great hall there are eight Osiride pillars, upward of thirty feet in height. The sides of the speos are carved with bass-reliefs, representing the conquests of Rameses the Great.

There are some sixteen smaller chambers, the suite terminating in the sanctuary, which contains an altar and four statues—the three deities, Amun re, Phre, and Phtah, with the king seated in their company.

Under the headings tombs and temples are comprised the chief architectural works of the Egyptians. Besides these there were one or two gigantic constructions, famous in antiquity, but which have now almost disappeared. Of these, the Labyrinth and the Lake Moeris were the most important. The former appears to have been an immense structure, half palace, half tomb, built by Amenemha III., of the twelfth dynasty. It was built on three sides of an open square, measuring about five hundred feet on the side, consisting of numerous chambers and courts, in two stories, one above and the other below the level of the ground. At the open end was placed a large pyramid, of which the ruins still remain. Herodotus admired the Labyrinth more than any other of the Egyptian buildings, declaring it to surpass the pyramids in labour and expense. Near by was the artificial Lake Moeris, formed to retain the Nile waters during the inundation, for the purpose of irrigating the country surrounding Memphis, during the dry season. It covered an immense area; tradition says 450 miles in circumference. The banks were fortified with massive masonry, and the waters distributed by means of locks and sluices.

The Egyptians appear as a civilized nation, having a scientific, artistic, and political knowledge of no mean order, at a time when the greater part of the world's inhabitants were but a step removed from the level of ignorant savages, and when, according to a generally accepted chronology, the world itself had existed but a few hundred years. The construction of the Pyramids reveals a building capacity which has rarely been rivalled, requiring not only immense mechanical power, but an accuracy of judgment and calculation in the adjustment of blocks of granite weighing many tons, not simply piled one above the other, but perfectly jointed and polished, and so disposed that passages and chambers were roofed over and their ceilings relieved from superincumbent weight by ingeniously contrived compartments, one above the other, and closed by sliding doors of monolithic stones, the handling of which could only have been successful by people well versed in the theories of equilibrium and support; and yet all this was done at a date which the best authorities agree in saying could not have been later than three thousand years before Christ. Their temples show an equally advanced erudition, and the paintings and hieroglyphics with which the walls of these buildings are adorned give a faithful representation of the customs of a people acquainted with the minor arts and sciences and the appliances requisite for agriculture.

The admiration with which we may regard the excellence of so ancient an art is tempered when we find that it contained no element of progress. The monuments of the eighteenth dynasty, though numerous and imposing, scarcely differ from those of the preceding period, and even in the days of the Ptolemys, who encouraged the native art, there was nothing attempted but a repetition of the old methods. From beginning to end the arts were so fettered by conventionality and dogmatic laws, opposed to originality or change, that the only improvements made were in mere mechanical execution.

A great prevailing thought seems to have actuated this people,—that of death and eternity. Their aim in erecting their buildings was to render them quasi-eternal, and by embalming the bodies of the dead they even sought to perpetuate the semblance of life. Their kings at the beginning of their reigns commenced the construction of their own sepulchres, employing hundreds of workmen and immense expenditure of the national funds for the purpose, and countless thousands passed their lives in hollowing temples in the mountain rock and in carrying huge blocks from great distances for the building of the pylons and hypostylic halls of the Nile, in which durability and massiveness were considered all-important.

Egyptian architecture, simply from the enormous scale of everything it produced, was always dignified and it had also the merit of severe simplicity; but mere size can scarcely be rated as an artistic quality of a high order, and on that account it cannot compare favourably with the art of the Greeks, who were probably inspired by what they saw in Egypt, but who, in their own work, succeeded in combining the qualities of majesty and beauty without resorting to the use of extraordinary materials.

III.

ASIATIC ARCHITECTURE.

IT would, perhaps, be reasonable to suppose that in India, where the Aryan race had its origin, the earliest traces of dawning art would be found. It has, however, been fairly well established that all remnants of very ancient art, which may have existed there in former times, have now virtually disappeared, and that at present there are no remains in Hindostan of a remoter antiquity than the second or third century before the Christian era.

The architecture of India loses much of its interest for us from the fact of its having had no influence upon the origin or development of the European styles of building, which, starting in Egypt and Assyria, formed a continuous chain, each linked with its predecessor and successor down to modern times.

The Indians were, in fact, never a migratory or colonizing race of people, and their architecture was a distinctly native production, executed in accordance with the rules laid down by the priests in their sacred books, having no affinity with the constructive principles of the Western world and showing no trace of the arts practised by Western nations, except in the slight resemblance of a few mouldings and fragments of sculpture.

The chief structures of the country are temples, pagodas, and dagobas, which are found in many different parts of the peninsular and adjacent islands, resembling each other in general style, but with some local peculiarities which have caused them to be usually classified in certain comprehensive divisions, of which the following are the most important:

The Buddhist style, including the stambhas or lats, a species of commemorative pillar, the stupas or topes, of which the best examples are found at Sarnath and Manikyala, and the viharas of Bengal.

The Dravidian style, exemplified in the temples of Chilambaram, Tanjore, Combaconum, and Madura, and the rock-cut temples of Mahavellipore, and those known as the Kylas at Ellora.

The Indo-Aryan, or Northern, comprising the temples of Kanaruc, Bhuwaneswur, Jajepur, and Cuttack, in the province of Orissa.

The stupas, or dagobas, were a form of structure specially erected for the purposes of Buddhist worship. They were sometimes built in the shape of a square tower upon rising ground, of which that at Sarnath, north of Benares, is the best known. The more important, however, are cylindrical and surmounted by a semi-circular dome. These are usually erected on artificial mounds or tumuli, and are constructed either with jointed stones or with rough blocks bedded in cement. The interiors are of solid masonry, with the exception of a small square chamber, used as a repository for sacred emblems, the walls of which are continued up to the top of the dome. The stupa at Manikyala, is of great size, being upward of eighty feet in height, and measuring some three hundred feet in circumference. The base of the building is in the form of a cylinder, six or seven feet high, supporting an attic decorated with pilasters; above this the walls recede, and are capped by a hemispherical dome. There are a great number of dagobas in Ceylon, in the mountainous districts. They are usually placed in a walled enclosure, and surrounded by commemorative pillars. Smaller constructions of the same description are found in the interior of some of the temples, being placed where the baldaquins, or altars, would be placed in Christian edifices.

The rock temples of India are of two classes, the one consisting of grottos hollowed in the mountain side, and the other of a series of monolithic buildings cut bodily out of the solid rock, and detached from the surrounding hill plateaus by wide excavated areas.

The former, resembling the speos of Egypt, consists of long galleries, divided into aisles by piers of the natural rock left at regular intervals to sustain the superincumbent mass. A recess or sanctuary is placed at one extremity, containing the statue of the divinity to whom the temple is dedicated. In some cases the interior is terminated by a semicircular apse with a hemispherical vault, and the entrance preceded by a vestibule containing votive figures, the whole forming a plan very similar to that of the Latin basilicas, which will be described in a subsequent chapter. The grottos are frequently excavated in several stories and connected by corridors and ramps.

The walls or sides are ornamented with rude sculptures, representing various forms of animal life and monstrous creations of native fancy. The piers or pillars are generally either square or octagonal, decorated with mouldings and flutings, and having well defined capitals and bases. The capitals usually support a stone beam or bracket, evidently in imitation of those used in wooden construction, in which a similar expedient would be employed to distribute the sustaining power over a wider surface than that directly above the column or post. This imitation of wooden forms, which we have already noticed in Egypt, is found universally in all ancient constructions showing that in nearly every country wooden architecture was employed before stone.

The group known as the Kylas of Ellora, is the finest example of the temples fashioned both inside and outside from the solid rock.

The whole edifice is monolithic and situated in an oblong court formed by a trench excavated "vivo saxo" on the four sides. The exterior surfaces are richly carved, and the piers shaped to represent elephants, lions, and fantastic creatures supporting the superstructure on their backs. The court is entered from a monumental porch, the upper story of which is connected with a small chapel by a bridge. This chapel is flanked by two colossal elephants, and by two columns or towers standing isolated on either side. A second bridge leads from this to the hall of Shiva, the chief room in the suite, which is divided by sixteen columns, with corresponding pilasters on the walls. At the farther extremity is the sanctuary containing the statue of the presiding divinity. Beyond this are open terraces, surrounded by chapels. The great hall is connected laterally with subterranean chambers in the surrounding cliffs, reached also from excavated corridors which follow the perimeter of the court, the mass above being sustained by square piers spaced at short distances apart.

The inside walls are decorated with bass-reliefs and the ceilings ornamented with stucco relievos, which were originally brilliantly painted. The height of the hall of Shiva is about fifty feet, the hillside opposite to it being about ninety feet high.

These temples may be said to be the most remarkable and unique architectural productions to be found anywhere. They are examples of long-continued perseverance and patience, and can only be the result of a preconceived design which must have been thoroughly studied in all its elaborate detail before the first stroke was given toward its realization. The unity of conception and execution exhibited in such works is truly wonderful, and it is not astonishing that the superstitious natives should attribute their creation to Visvakarma, the heavenly architect. On the other hand, there are but few practical lessons to be learned from their examination. Such methods are not possible in our day, nor if so, would they be desirable. Architecture of this kind is scarcely more than wholesale sculpture, and as such can in no sense compare favourably with the grace of form and scientific construction which we see in the works of Greek and Gothic artists.

The Pagodas are the most important of the buildings constructed with jointed materials. They consist of vast enclosures containing numerous religious and domestic edifices. There are often double or triple series of enclosing walls of great height and thickness. The sides are usually placed so as to face the points of the compass and each contains a monumental entrance, richly sculptured, and adorned with bands of embossed copper.

The chief buildings within are, the temple proper, or vimana and a number of hypostylic halls with small sanctuaries dedicated to different divinities.

The form of the vimana differs in the North and South of India. In both cases it is pyramidal, but while in the Southern temples the plan is rectangular and the elevations marked by a series of horizontal stories and mouldings, in the North the exterior surfaces are convex and the outlines curved, showing vertical instead of horizontal divisions. The lower story, containing the idol, is usually a hollow cube of granite, and serves as a base to the pyramid above, which is most frequently built of brick with stucco facing.

The halls are composed of a great number of columns of varied design, placed in parallel rows. The ceilings are formed by stone beams or slabs resting upon the columns. The central aisle is frequently wider than the others and is roofed over by a corbelled vault.

A tank of sacred water surrounded by an open colonnade is not uncommonly placed within the enclosure, the waters being used by the infirm for the healing properties which they are supposed to contain.

The pagodas of Tanjore, Combaconum, and Madura are among the finest and most celebrated. They were built between the fifth and eleventh centuries of the Christian era, and should hardly, therefore, be described among the ancient buildings of the world, were it not that they are linked in with the chain of the older Indian art too closely to be separated from it.

In the period corresponding to the Middle Ages of Europe, Mahometan architecture was introduced in India and many beautiful buildings were erected in a new style blending the foreign art with the native ideas and taste, but offering a marked contrast to that which preceded it.

Although China was one of the oldest of civilized countries it contains but few monuments of great antiquity. The temples and palaces, being built of wood, were exposed to fire and decay, and were often pulled down and rebuilt. With the exception of the great wall and of the numerous bridges crossing rivers or arms of the sea, there are no important stone constructions to be found there.

The latter are formed of huge granite piers, spanned by massive stone lintels, requiring the united labour of thousands of men to convey them from the quarries to their destination and to set them in place. In the mountains the ravines are bridged by iron chains suspended from cliff to cliff.

The great wall was built as a frontier protection, and extended the entire length of the boundaries of the country. It has always been kept in repair, although obviously absurd as a fortification in modern times. It is of great thickness, and upward of twenty feet in height. The foundations are of stone, and the upper part of brick with stone facing, the joints of which are extremely accurate. At short intervals there are towers, placed so that the middle distance between any two is within arrow-shot.

Chinese wooden buildings are all much alike, whether temples or palaces. As a rule, they have but one or two stories; they are surrounded by porticos, consisting of wooden columns mounted on stone bases, without capitals, which are replaced by a species of bracket. The roofs project considerably, and their angles are turned up, this form being undoubtedly borrowed from the old tent habitations, which were composed of hides stretched tightly on bamboos. The tiles with which they are covered are semicylindrical in shape and are enamelled with bright colour.

The celebrated taas, or Buddhist towers, are of similar construction. They are generally octagonal, and from six to ten stories high. Each story is set back from the one below, and has a balcony and projecting roof, with bells hung in the angles. The walls are covered with tiles or paintings. A high staff is placed on the top and connected with angles of the roof by chains.

The tower of Nankin, known as the Porcelain Tower, was the most famous. It was erected in 1431, and but recently destroyed.

The Chinese have always excelled in artificial or landscape gardening. In this work they build airy bridges, with open-work balustrades, pavilions highly ornamented and enriched with painting and gilding, and boundary walls with circular openings, disclosing vistas of great beauty.

Their commemorative gateways are of interest, as they have a central opening and a smaller one on each side, like the Roman triumphal arches; the heads are square, however, with brackets in the corners. The upper parts are ornamented with figures in relief and inscriptions recording the virtues of persons to whose memory they are dedicated.

Although communication existed between China and the countries bordering upon the Mediterranean from remote ages, Chinese architecture, like the Indian, was without influence upon that of Europe. It is only in Western Asia that the first forms of building are discernible, which were subsequently imitated or followed in European constructions. The most important of these are situated in Mesopotamia, the fertile region comprised between the Tigris and the Euphrates.

The political histories of Assyria, Babylon, and Persia are generally treated separately, but the architecture of each belongs to one style, which may be called the Assyrian, for its distinguishing characteristics remain the same in all the great cities which were in turn the capitals of reconstructed kingdoms and empires.

It may be considered in four chronological divisions: In ancient Babylon, from 2234 B.C. to 1520 B.C., at Wurka and Mugheyr; in Nineveh, from the fourteenth to the seventh century B.C., at Nimrod, Khorsabad, and Koyoundjik; in the second Babylon, during the seventh century and after the capture of the latter by Cyrus in the year 538 B.C., in Persia, at Persepolis, Passargadæ, and Susa. A renaissance of the art may be traced in Sassanian buildings erected eight centuries later.

The citadels, palaces, and other important structures of these cities were usually built upon artificial mounds or terraces, strengthened by massive walls.

The materials used were bituminous bricks, cemented with bitumen, slabs of gypsum anchored with copper nails and bands, and timber for roofs and columns. Stone and gypsum or ababaster were employed in Nineveh and in the cities of Persia. In Babylon the only available material was bituminous clay, and consequently all the buildings there were built of brick. At the present day nothing remains of these but irregular mounds, from which but little can be gathered toward an understanding of what their appearance was when entire.

Wood was probably used to a great extent, and was naturally most easily destroyed by the fire of invading armies. The roofs, formed of thick layers of earth carried on beams, in falling in, buried the lower portions of buildings, and it is probably due to this fact that the bass-reliefs have been preserved.

The surfaces of the bricks were frequently enamelled in colours, and the woodwork was probably brilliantly painted, as traces of pigments have been found upon the more durable materials.

But little was known of Assyrian art prior to 1843, when the excavations of Botta, the French consul at Mosul, followed soon after by those conducted by Layard, brought to light many ruined buildings, in which bass-reliefs, inscribed stones and metals, and other important relics were found, enabling historians to form a consecutive account of the government, warfare, and arts practised by a people whose cities have lain buried and whose very name has almost been forgotten for over two thousand years.

The explorations were made in Nimrod, Koyoundjik, and Khorsabad. The palace of Asshur-banipal, erected at Nimrod, in the ninth century B.C., is situated upon a terrace, or platform, approached by a wide staircase, and preceded by two gates decorated with winged bulls.

These winged bulls, or lions, were placed as the guardian deities, at the portals of all the great Assyrian palaces, after the manner of the Egyptian sphinxes, not standing isolated like these, however, but built into the masonry, one side or the front and one side only, being carved. The head was human, with long beard and hair, and surmounted by a helmet, the wings large and proportioned to the body. As Sir Henry Layard remarks, it would have been difficult to find more fitting symbols to express at once the wisdom, power, and ubiquity of a supreme being.

The chief apartments of the palace are a large assembly hall, 152 feet in length by 30 feet in width, and a number of smaller chambers and banqueting-halls, ranged around an open court. The walls of the great hall were decorated with bass-reliefs, representing triumphal processions, carved upon slabs of gypsum eight feet in height.

The palace of Esarhaddon, erected in the seventh century, on the same terrace, contains a large hall,

165 by 62 feet, divided in its length by a wall, surmounted by a gallery of columns. One of the only well-preserved ramps which has been discovered was that leading to this palace.

At Koyoundjik, opposite Mosul, the palace of Sennacherib was found at the Southwest corner of a mound a mile and a half in circumference. It contained a vast number of courts and halls, decorated with bass-reliefs and winged bulls, and two colossal statues.

The palace of Sargon at Khorsabad, erected in the year 704 B.C., is among the best preserved. Like the others it is placed upon an artificial terrace, enclosed by a wall a mile long on each side. It was defended by a citadel of eight towers with doors flanked by winged bulls. The palace was reached by a long, narrow passage leading to a court and entered through three great gates. The bulls of the central portal were 19 feet high. On each side were two bulls, 13 feet high, with the figure of a giant strangling a lion between them.

The halls and chambers were grouped around two great courts measuring about 350 by 200 feet. The hareem formed a separate set of buildings, as did also the stables and outhouses. The walls were of great thickness, evidently for coolness. They were decorated with slabs of alabaster, enamelled tiles, and designs painted on stucco.

There has been much speculation on the method of roofing these rooms, some believing that circular vaults were employed and others that wooden beams, supported on wooden columns, similar to the stone ones found in Persian palaces, were used for this purpose. The latter theory seems the more probable, as the local manner of building is the same as this at the present day. No traces of columns remain, however, and the spans are in many cases too great to be roofed by single pieces of timber. One of the most interesting discoveries made at Khorsabad was the gate of the city, the jambs supporting a semicircular arch over a span of eighteen feet. The gate was a double one having two separate passages, one for vehicles and the other for pedestrians: the marks of chariot-wheels still remaining in the pavement of the former. The sides were ornamented with winged bulls, and the archivolts of the arches were decorated with blue and yellow designs in enamelled tiles.

It had been long supposed that the Etruscans were the first to make use of the true semicircular arch (*i.e.*, formed of wedge-shaped stones or bricks, with joints radiating to a common centre), but this discovery, and the finding of pointed arches in the sewers of Babylon, by Layard, places the date when both these expedients were known, at a much remoter period, though even these are probably much later than the examples found in Egypt.

No complete example of a Chaldean temple has been found, but there are several the lower stories of which are sufficiently well preserved to give an accurate idea of their size and details, and in the tomb of Cyrus at Passagardæ, in Persia, we have probably a model on a small scale of one of these buildings when entire. This tomb consists of a platform of six steps, eighteen feet high, surmounted by a rectangular chamber. The latter has a doorway and a ridged roof abutting against pediments.

It has been surmised that all the temples were like this, consisting of a chamber or cella built on the summit of a several-storied structure, each story being either concentric and reached by a ramp winding around the four sides or placed farther to one side than that immediately below it and approached by straight flights of stairs.

The oldest is probably that at Wurka, dating as far back as 2000 B.C., known as the Bowariyeh. There are the remains of two stories, the lower occupying about 200 square feet. It is probable that a third story or a cella was placed above these, but nothing positive can be said on the subject, owing to the extremely ruinous condition of the building. The temple of Birs Nimroud, probably identical with the tower of Babel, is in a more satisfactory condition, the upper story having been preserved by a process of vitrification. The lowest story occupies a square measuring 272 feet on the side, each of the upper ones, of which it is supposed there were originally six, being 42 feet less.

For the materials used in its construction we have

the scriptural authority : " Go to, let us make brick and burn them thoroughly. And they had brick for stone, and slime had they for mortar " (Gen. xi.) ; slime being probably bitumen.

M. Place discovered the remains of a tower at Khorsabad, with a winding ramp, which he thinks was originally seven stories in height. The walls were strengthened with buttresses and decorated with sunken panels, and from traces of colour found upon them it has been supposed that each floor was painted in a different hue. The area covered by the base is about one hundred and fifty square feet, and the total height was probably one hundred and thirty-five feet.

The ruins of Persepolis are the best preserved of the ancient Persian buildings, those at Susa and Passagardæ being in too bad a condition to offer much that is interesting.

They are situated in the plain of Mardacht, upon a terrace partly formed of masonry, and partly cut in the rock of the adjoining range of hills. The wall is composed of huge blocks of stone fitted together without mortar, but with the finest of joints. The terrace is reached by a splendid double flight of steps, upward of twenty feet in width, and on a grade easy enough to permit of the passage of long processions without interruption. At the head of the stairs is a propylæum, or outer gate, flanked by colossal human-headed bulls. Beyond this, a second staircase, ornamented with a triple row of bass-reliefs, gives access to the Chehil Minar, or great hall of Xerxes.

This building occupies a rectangle about three hundred and fifty feet long by three hundred in width. It consists chiefly of a central hall and three lateral porticos, the roofs of which were sustained by 72 columns, 36 in the hall and 12 in each of the porches.

Thirteen of these are still standing, and the position of all the others is well defined by broken bases or shafts. They are of two different kinds, the one having a capital composed of double-headed bulls, and the other a capital with volutes, not placed horizontally as we see them in classical columns, but vertically and resting on a complicated series of mouldings. These last may have been also surmounted by the double-headed bulls, as without such an addition the columns are shorter than the others, which measure 67 feet 4 inches. The beams which they sustained, rested upon the body of the bull between the two heads.

The shafts of the columns at Persepolis are fluted and taper upward from the bases, which are elaborately ornamented with mouldings.

It is probable that the Greek Ionic capital was derived directly from the Persian voluted model, as the order originated in the Greek colony in Asia Minor.

The Chehil Minar is the finest building on the platform, the other halls of Darius and Xerxes being smaller, and though a hall containing 100 columns has been found, it is inferior in height, the total altitude not exceeding twenty-five feet.

The hall of Darius contained sixteen columns, forming a square, preceded by a portico with eight more. The walls have long since disappeared, but the façade of the building is reproduced upon the face of the rock-cut tomb of Darius in the neighbouring hill called Naksh-i-Rustam, so that a restoration of the structure as it originally appeared is easily made.

This tomb shows the four front columns of the porch with double-headed capitals, sustaining an entablature, above this is placed an attic decorated with bass-reliefs and a figure is represented standing on the top in the act of sacrificing on an altar.

The stone buildings of Persia are generally supposed to be reproductions of the wooden constructions of Assyria, as the character of the art is similar in both, the bass-reliefs and winged bulls of Persepolis being practically identical with those of Nineveh.

We find no traces of Assyrian art for several centuries after the erection of the buildings just described, though it is probable that it had influence in all Eastern edifices erected during the interval, not only in Asia, but in Greece and later in Byzance. There was evidently a revival of Assyrian taste during the dynasty of Sassanian kings who reigned between the third and seventh centuries of our era. The remnants of their palaces are found at Firouzabad, Al Hadhr, Serbistan, Ctesiphon, and Mashita, where we find large halls vaulted and domed and ornamented in a manner directly traceable to the ancient buildings in Assyria. The chief peculiarity of these structures lies in the use of the horse-shoe or elliptical arch, which is found nowhere else. The porch of the Tak-Kesra at Ctesiphon consists of a great elliptical tunnel-vault, 115 feet deep, 85 feet high, over a span of 72 feet.

There is more or less Roman influence in the details of the Sassanian palaces, but it is not altogether certain whether the knowledge of domical construction which they exhibit was derived from, or was not itself parent to, Byzantine art.

Comparatively little is known concerning this Assyrian style, but it contains interesting elements, and it may be that its constructive forms are susceptible of a greater development in our own time.

Asia Minor, Palestine, and Cyprus are fields covered with the evidences of the glory of past ages, but the ruin and desolation everywhere is complete. The case of the temple of Jerusalem, where not one stone remains upon another, applies in most instances in places which have formerly been great cities, filled with magnificent buildings which were their pride in the day of their prosperity.

The temple of Solomon was situated upon Mount Moriah, and was built to accommodate the Levites, to offer a place of assembly for the people, and as a temple for the worship of the priests. The two sanctuaries were richly decorated with polished cedar and gold, with columns and cornices of bronze, and divided by linen curtains embroidered with purple and scarlet.

The peculiar formation of the hill upon which it was built, required immense walls of the most substantial character to be raised from the valley below to enlarge its summit, so as to afford sufficient space for the erection of the various courts. "It was built of stone, made ready before it was brought thither; so that there was neither hammer, nor axe, nor any tool of iron heard in the house while it was in building" (2 Kings vi., 7).

The temple itself is supposed to have been 60 cubits long, the porch 20 cubits, the Holy place 20 cubits; the width was 20 cubits and the height 30 cubits. The porch, however, was 120 cubits high. (The cubit is estimated to equal from 10 to 20 inches.)

The temple underwent several profanations, and at last was utterly destroyed in the reign of Jedekiah by Nebuchadnezzar, 580 B.C. After laying in ruins 42 years, the foundation of the second temple was laid by Zerubbabel and in breadth and height was double that of Solomon's. This second temple was plundered and profaned by Antiochus Epiphanes, and afterward rebuilt by Herod. It was considerably larger than its predecessor and was made of marble and of the most costly workmanship. It became the admiration and envy of the world, but, as our Lord predicted (Mark xiii., 2), it was completely demolished by Titus, A.D. 70.

Many restorations of the temples of the Greek colonists in Ionia have been attempted, but they are based on historical descriptions, inscriptions on coins, and other uncertain records, and are too conjectural to be accepted as accurate. There are, in fact, but few architectural remains sufficiently well preserved to be of interest to the architect, excepting the temples at Baalbek and Palmyra which are of the Roman period.

There are several groups of tombs, the most important being in Lycia.

These are of interest, as they illustrate more completely the transition between wooden and stone building than any other examples. There are two kinds, the one consisting of sarcophagi standing isolated, and the other of excavations in the mountainsides. The former are composed of a stylobate or pedestal, serving as a base to a coffer ornamented with uprights and crosspieces and panelled doors imitating exactly a wooden original. The roofs are curved, having in section the form of a pointed arch, being probably the earliest instances of its employment as a decorative feature.

The tombs cut in the face of the rock are of a similar description, having the same carpentry framework. The upper parts are terminated by a low pediment or by a row of stone logs supporting a horizontal moulding.

Later on during the Greek occupation, these wooden forms were abandoned and replaced by porticos of the Ionic order.

In various parts of Asia Minor, there are remains of tombs similar to these erected by the Pelasgi and Etruscans, which will be described in another chapter.

IV.

GREECE.

THE oldest architectural works in Greece are those erected by the Cyclopes or Pelasgi, a race who came originally from Lycia, and moved gradually Westward, peopling successively the islands of the Grecian Archipelago, the Peloponnesus, Sicily, and Italy. At Tiryns and Mycenæ, in the province of Argolis, are to be seen the most remarkable remains of the buildings of this people, which were always grouped together in walled cities, serving as strongholds to protect the inhabitants of the province from the wild tribes with whom they came in contact. These cities were generally placed upon a rocky eminence, difficult of access and commanding a view of the surrounding country.

There are remains of high walls at Tiryns built of huge stones extracted from a neighbouring quarry and put together without cement or mortar, the interstices being filled with smaller stones. From the fallen blocks lying scattered at their base it is estimated that they originally measured sixty feet in height.

At intervals these walls are pierced by triangular doors and windows, the sides of which are curved, forming arches obtained by corbelled or overlapping instead of wedged stones. These Cyclopean constructions date from the seventeenth century before Christ.

The Acropolis of Mycenæ is entered by a doorway formed of two vertical monoliths of great size supporting a lintel, and called the Gate of the Lions, from the carving above, representing two rampant lions separated by an engaged column.

This city was surrounded by high fortified walls, and contained a place of assembly for the people and rude habitations, the remains of which are still visible. There is also still to be seen a conical or bee-hive-like structure, commonly called the Treasury of Atreus. This cone is formed by overlapping stones, curving gradually until they meet at the top of the vault, which is capped by a large block. The doorway by which it is entered is composed of slanting jambs of stone, sustaining a massive lintel. This lintel is relieved from direct weight above by a triangular opening, obtained by a similar process of corbelling. The Cyclopean remains are of interest to architects chiefly on account of this system of corbelled vaulting employed in their construction, which would never have been adopted had their builders been acquainted with the voussoir principle.

Dr. Schliemann has recently excavated the Acropolis of Mycenæ, and found there many interesting objects of gold and pottery. Bronze nails with flat heads have also been found within the Treasury of Atreus, which were evidently used to attach copper plates with which the interior was lined. Pausanias speaks of a similar treasury belonging to King Minyas, at Orchomenos, and other remains of the same description have been discovered in different parts of the Morea, bearing a resemblance to the ruined cities of Etruria.

In fact, the various tumuli found in Western Europe, Sardinia, Sicily, Greece, and Asia are all of the same type, and were a form commonly adopted by the ancient nations.

When we come to the epoch preceding Roman architecture, we will examine the character of Etruscan buildings, which were similar in many respects to the works of the Pelasgi; at present the subject of most interest is that of the great century of Greek art, for it marks the transition from Crude Art, to which belongs all that has preceded, to Fine Art, in which the Greeks excelled.

Greek buildings were erected according to the rules of three systems or orders, of the origin and character of which Vitruvius gives the following account, which, if not strictly accurate, is at least as reasonable as some of the versions which have been advanced. "Dorus, King of the Peloponnesus, having had a temple erected to Juno, in Argos, it was built by chance in the manner which we call Doric;

afterward, in several other towns, other temples were built in this same order, having no established rule for the proportions of their architecture. About the same period the Athenians established several colonies in Asia Minor under the guidance of Ion, and they called the country which he occupied Ionia. These colonists built Doric temples there at first, of which the chief was that of Apollo, but as they did not know what proportion to give to the columns, they sought the means of making them at once strong enough to sustain the building, and of rendering them at the same time agreeable to the eye. For this they took the measure of a man's foot as the sixth part of his height, and on this measure formed their column, giving it six diameters.*

"Some time afterward, wishing to build a temple to Diana, they endeavoured to find a new method, equally beautiful and more appropriate to their purpose. They imitated the delicacy of a woman's form; they heightened the columns, gave them a base like the twisted cords which bind a sandal; they carved volutes in the capital to represent that portion of the hair which falls to the right and left of the head; they put circles and rings on the columns to imitate the rest of the hair which is braided and caught up on the back of women's heads; and

---

* We have already seen that there are columns at Beni Hassan, in Egypt, resembling so closely the Greek Doric, that it is reasonable to suppose that the Greeks borrowed their conception of the order from the Egyptians and refined it.

by flutings they imitated the folds of the dress. And this order, invented by the Ionians, took the name of Ionic.

"The Corinthian column represents the delicacy of a young girl, at the age when the figure is slender and best suited to the display of ornaments which may add to her natural beauty. The invention of its capital is due to the following incident: A young girl of Corinth, who was about to marry, having died, her nurse placed some little vases which she had been fond of during her life, in a basket on her tomb, and, in order that the weather should not spoil them, she placed a tile on the basket. This, having been laid accidentally over an acanthus-root, it came to pass, when the leaves began to grow, that the stems of the plant crept up the sides of the basket and, meeting the corners of the tile, were forced to curve downward, and to take the form of volutes. Callimachus, a sculptor and architect, struck by the harmonious result, imitated it in the capitals of columns which he subsequently made in Corinth, establishing on this model the proportions of the Corinthian order."

At this stage it is necessary to explain briefly that an order consists of a column, the pedestal upon which it stands, and the entablature, or top member, which it supports. The column is subdivided into the capital, or head; the shaft, or body; and the base, or foot. The entablature has likewise three divisions: the architrave, or beam sustained by the

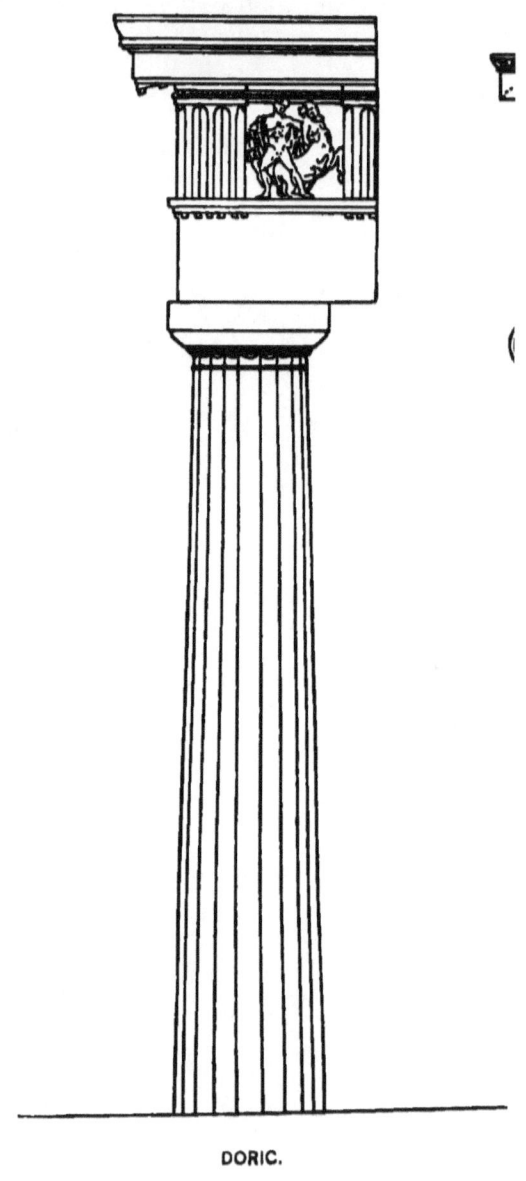

DORIC.

THE

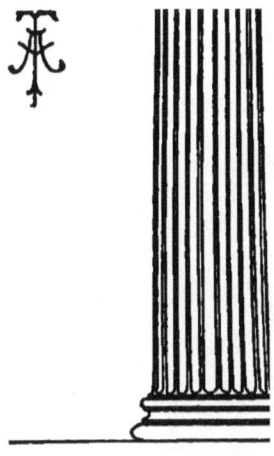

CORINTHIAN.

columns; the frieze, or space occupied by the cross-beams; and the cornice, or line of stone marking the extremity of the rafters. These were originally made of wood and subsequently imitated in stone.*

The Greek Doric column had no base and rested upon a series of steps in place of the pedestal. The ends of the cross-beams were marked upon the frieze by a projection, upon which were cut three grooves into which the rain-water ran and fell in drops to the ground. These drops were represented in stone underneath, completing an ornament which was called a triglyph (meaning in Greek, three grooves). The spaces intervening between the triglyphs were called metopes. The inclination of the sides of the roof formed the lines of the triangular termination which we call the pediment.

The Greeks employed three methods in their Doric, namely, the hexametric, heptametric, and octometric, that is, a proportion of six, seven, and eight diameters to the height.

We have seen what were the component parts of the Ionic and Corinthian orders in the quotation from Vitruvius.

In Greek temples the shafts of the columns not only tapered considerably, but the vertical lines of an entire building inclined to imaginary points deter-

---

* Viollet le Duc maintained that the Greek buildings were in no sense an imitation of wooden constructions, but gave no very satisfactory explanation of the origin of their component parts. It is perhaps best to conclude that they were adaptations of pre-existing edifices to new materials.

mined by the intersection of lines following the inclination of the end columns. The mass was thus in the form of the frustum of a pyramid, being intentionally so designed to bind the parts of the building together in a manner to withstand effectually the oscillation caused by earthquakes, which occur frequently in this region.

The city of Athens contained numerous examples of each of these orders, and a brief account of the buildings of that city will be the best means of showing their principal characteristics.

The city proper, in which were the chief temples, was built upon a rocky hill rising from the valley of the Illysus, lying between the mountain-chains of Pentelicus and Hymettus, and situated about five miles from the port of Phalerum, on the Gulf of Ægina. This Acropolis (rock city) is approached by a broad flight of stairs leading to the Propylæum, or outer gate, with high pedestals on each side which were formerly surmounted by equestrian statues.

The Propylæum is composed of a porch of six Doric columns, giving access to a large vestibule flanked by two outer halls. This vestibule is divided by a flight of steps, placed between six Ionic columns on pedestals, supporting nine marble beams or architraves which carry the weight of the roof.

Beyond is a second porch, opening on the plateau of the Acropolis by means of five doors of different proportions. The lintel of the central or largest door measures 23 feet, while the architraves are 17 feet in length and of single stones.

The Athenians prided themselves greatly upon the vestibule of the Propylæum, and believed Pericles, by whose direction the building was erected, to have been divinely inspired. The details and proportions of the two orders here combined are of great beauty, and show the most refined study. From the farther porch, the Parthenon (meaning in Greek, virgin), or temple of Minerva, is seen to the right, exhibiting a fine perspective view of its North and West elevations.

The temple is raised upon a platform surrounded by steps, and is rectangular in form, composed of a cella, or oblong room, surrounded by an open portico. It measures 228 by 101 feet, having eight Doric columns on the front and seventeen on the flank, inclusive of the corner ones.

Ictinus and Callicrates were the architects, under the general supervision of Phidias, who designed the gold and ivory figure of Minerva within.

The Doric is of the hexametric order, having an approximate proportion of six diameters of the column to its height.

The pediments of the Parthenon were decorated with rich carvings in high relief, representing, in the one, the presentation of Minerva to the assembled gods by her father Jupiter, and in the other, the contest of Minerva and Neptune for the naming of the city.

In the metopes were depicted the battles of the Athenians with the Centaurs, and scenes in the lives of Perseus, Theseus, and Hercules, in the admirable sculpture of Phidias.

The building stood almost intact from the fifth century before Christ to the seventeenth century of our era, when it suffered greatly from Venetian artillery, and in modern times its richest sculpture was torn from it under the Turkish régime, by order of Lord Elgin, who obtained permission from the authorities to remove it to the British Museum. One of the ships containing the marbles was sunk off Cape Matapan. Even in its ruined condition the Parthenon stands to-day a great example of the finest architecture the world has known.

On the plateau of the Acropolis are the three contiguous temples of Pandrosus, Erictheus, and Minerva Polias, and the temple of the Wingless Victory (Niké Apteros), of the Ionic order.

The temple of Pandrosus is virtually a porch attached to the larger temple of Erictheus. It is composed of six female figures or caryatides upon a high base, supporting an entablature without frieze. These figures are of exceeding grace and beauty, and are models of the sculptor's art. The single cella was probably divided into three, to which access was had separately by the several porches. The ceilings of these temples are flat and decorated with sunken panels, ornamented with egg and dart moulds. According to Diodorus Sicculus, the temple of Erictheus was erected in his honour by the Athenians, in gratitude for his having instructed them in the worship of Ceres, Goddess of Agriculture. While Pausanias states that it contained the miraculous spring created by Neptune, who shared in its dedication.

There are three windows in the wall of the cella —unusual features in Greek architecture—and the levels of the temples are different, evidently so arranged, with a view to distinguish them the more completely.

The temple of the Wingless Victory is supposed to have been erected where Ægeus fell from the wall upon seeing the black sails of his son's ship returning after his victory over the Minotaur. Others again assert that it was built without reference to site and so called because the Athenians considered victory would never leave them, and consequently needed no wings. The temple is composed of a cella and two porches of four columns each, supporting a beautifully decorated entablature.

At the base of the Acropolis stood the resident portion of the city, containing also other temples and public buildings, which are still standing. The most important are the temple of Theseus, the Tower of the Winds, the theatre of Bacchus, and the monument of Lysicrates. Besides these there are many Roman buildings, but they belong to a subsequent period.

Plutarch says that the Athenians under Cimon erected the temple of Theseus on his return from Crete, and that it is of older construction than the temple of Minerva. It has six columns in the front and thirteen in flank, supporting marble beams the extremities of which rest on the inner wall and correspond on the other with the triglyphs on the outer face. The metopes had carvings representing the exploits of Theseus. The temple stands at the base of the Acropolis to the North; it is similar to the Parthenon in many respects, being of the same Doric order, though less rich in sculpture. It is the best preserved of all the monuments, having suffered but little during the twenty-two centuries it has existed.

The Tower of the Winds, erected by Adronichus Cyrrhastes, is an octagonal structure surmounted by a frieze, upon which the eight winds of heaven are carved in allegorical figures. The roof is a pyramid of marble slabs and was at one time surmounted by a bronze triton holding a switch, which answered the purpose of a vane, but has since disappeared. The building was used as a water-clock.

The choragic monument of Lysicrates, commonly called the Lantern of Demosthenes, is a circular structure of the Corinthian order. The spaces intervening between its six columns are closed by panels of a single stone upon which trivets are carved. The stone roof is decorated with scales

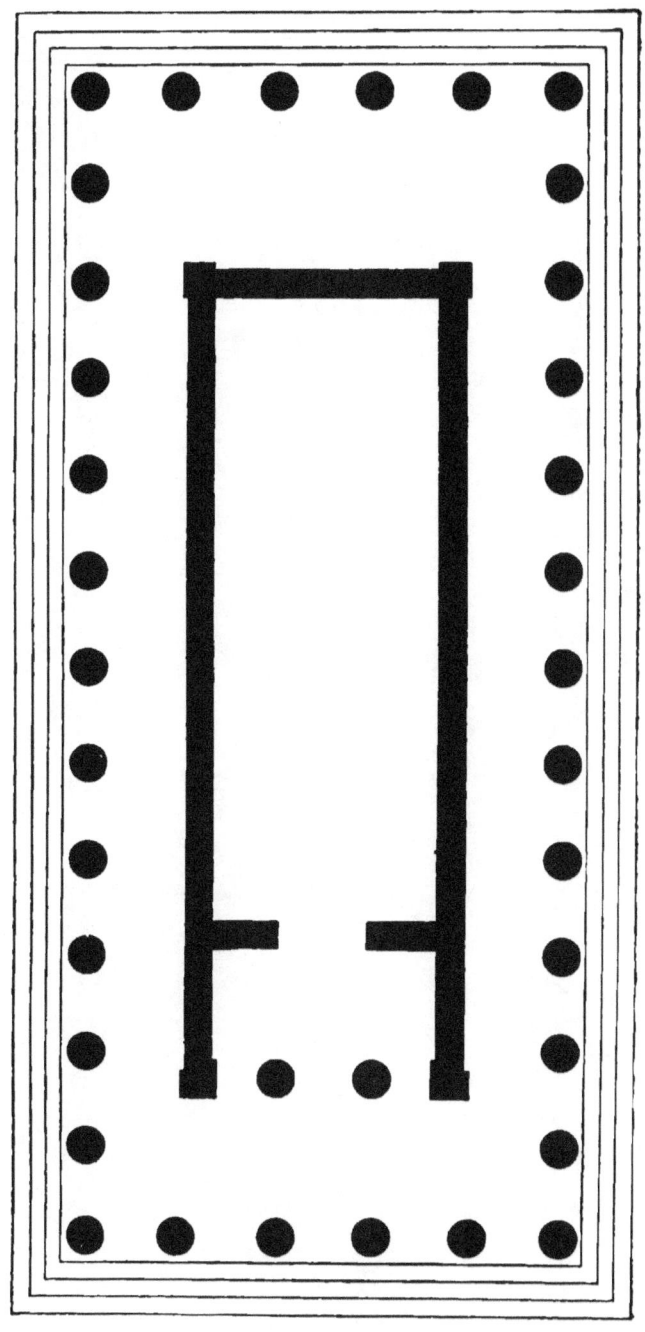

PLAN OF THE TEMPLE OF THESEUS AT ATHENS.

and surmounted by a finial of delicate workmanship. On this was placed the tripod of the choir which had been successful in the Olympian contest of the year 375 B.C., according to inscription.

There are other Corinthian buildings scattered throughout Greece, but this is generally taken to be the best example and its proportions followed. The carvings of the frieze depict the exploits of Hercules, who is represented clothed in the traditional lion's skin.

On the opposite slope of the hill are the ruined chairs and benches of the theatre of Bacchus, fronting an open stage. In building a theatre, the Northern slope of a hillside was generally selected for the site, in order to avoid the direct solar rays. Seats were provided for the audience by cutting circular tiers in the rock and a marble stage, profusely ornamented, was erected facing them. The stage was raised in order that the orchestra might not interfere with the view of the actors, and a portico adjoining it, served as a promenade during the intervals in the performance.

The stadium, or circus, of Athens was formed in this way, taking in plan the shape of a horse-shoe. It was here that the public games and races took place, the upper or circular end being occupied by the seats of the judges. It belongs, however, to a later period, having been constructed in the time of the Roman Emperor Hadrian. A few years ago the King of Greece caused the stadium to be excavated, and several marble chairs and seats were discovered.

Each city of importance possessed a Palæstra, or gymnasium, in which were rooms for bathing in hot or cold water, for the wrestlers to anoint themselves with oil and fine dust, and a school for young lads. The building was enclosed by a portico and surrounded by pleasure-grounds in which the public exercises took place.

The private dwellings were of one story in height, surmounted by terraces and divided by courts. The women's apartments were separated from the men's, and the larger houses contained banqueting-halls with accommodation for musicians and singers. The furniture consisted of tables in wood and choice stone, vases, candelabra, tripods in bronze, and rich Oriental carpets.

Externally the houses were painted brilliantly and decorated with wreaths, garlands, and arms. Outside the entrance door stood the statue of the god of the household—Jupiter, Minerva, or Mercury.

The richer citizens preferred country villas to city residences, which they surrounded with ornamental gardens and woods. The groves of the Academy where Plato held his school in the shade of the olives, outside the city gates, are probably the most celebrated of the latter.

The dead were buried in necropoli without the city, and their place of interment marked by tombs in the form of pyramids or funeral pyres, or more simply by a stella, or upright tablet, inscribed with the name and virtues of the deceased, and upon which were carved scenes in his life. In the colonies in Asia Minor the system of excavating chambers in the rock was adopted, the entrance to them being marked by Ionic columns supporting entablatures and pediments.

The public buildings of Athens were built of white marble from the island of Paros and the mountain quarries of Pentelicus, resembling in its fracture the purest loaf-sugar. The sun and rain have stained them to a tawny red during the many ages which have passed over them, and nearly all trace of the various dyes, with which they are supposed to have been coloured, has disappeared to-day.

The Greeks built their walls of bonded masonry, the vertical joints coming in the centres of the stones above and below, and they were frequently additionally strengthened by metal anchors. In walls of unusual thickness it was customary to construct the inside and outside faces first and fill the intervening spaces with loose stones and mortar, with an occasional through stone to connect the parts and bind them together.

The joints were sometimes emphasized by grooves, but this ornament was used more frequently in Roman work.

Until its introduction by the Romans the arch was rarely, if ever, employed, and the limit of intercolumniation was restricted by the necessity of finding stones of sufficient length to form the architraves.

The roofs were generally of wood, covered with terra-cotta tiles or sheet metal, and left open at intervals for the admission of light. This is, however, a disputed point, as the wood, being perishable, has left no positive proofs of the method employed. It appears that an awning or sail was stretched over these openings when services were being held. It is probable that in many instances there was no light admitted, except that from the entrance door. The effect of a religious ceremony performed in the temples by the artificial light of torches, with the flickering fires from the tripods and votive stands reflected upon the ivory and gold of the statues, and the smoke wreathing weirdly above the heads of the assembled multitude, must have been infinitely more impressive than if lit by the colder light of day.

The Greek colonists carried the principles of their architecture with them, leaving monuments of their genius wherever they established themselves. Of the temple of Diana, at Ephesus, nothing but a few fluted drums and scattered fragments remain to-day. It was the most magnificent temple of the Ionic order, erected with lavish expenditure, and decorated within with panels of cedar wood. It was burned and pillaged by the Persians.

At Agrigentum, in Sicily, and Pæstum, in Southern Italy, there are several Doric temples of massive proportions. Of these the temples of Concord, Jupiter, and Neptune are the most notable. The columns are shorter and their capitals broader than the Athenian type, and in one instance there are two orders superposed, within the cella, to support the roof.

The Greeks erected buildings in many parts of Southern Europe, in Asia Minor, and in Egypt, and in later times, even under the Roman conquest, they remained the masters of the arts, teaching their principles and supervising the erection of the monuments of Rome. The race was, indeed, peculiarly endowed with a genius for creating the beautiful, for though we have but scant information on the subject of Greek painting, we have preserved to us examples of sculpture which have never been surpassed or even equalled, and in architecture, though many more elaborate buildings have since been erected, nothing has ever been produced worthy of comparison with the harmonious proportions and majestic simplicity of the temples of Attica.

V.

ETRURIA AND ROME.

ETRURIA was peopled, from remote ages, by the indigenous inhabitants, and by colonizing races from Asia and Greece.

To the latter may be attributed the chief architectural works of the country; the ancient Etruscan walled cities resembling, in their general construction, those of Tiryns and Mycenæ.

Judging from the remains found upon the soil at the present day, the Etruscans used their knowledge of the laws of building principally in the erection of tombs. Of temples there now remain no traces; but, according to Vitruvius, they were composed, as a rule, of the rectangular chamber, or cella, of the Greeks, which was divided into three parts, and preceded by a porch of Tuscan columns. The origin of the latter he describes as follows:

"The Greek colonists, having brought to Etruria, the Tuscany of to-day, their acquaintance with the proportions of the Doric order, which was the only one as yet used in Greece, they employed this order there during a long period, in the same manner as in the country where it originated; but finally they changed it in several respects; they lengthened the column, and added a base to it; they altered the capital, simplified the entablature, and, thus changed, it was adopted by the Romans, under the name of the Tuscan order."

Etruscan tombs varied with the nature of the districts in which they were erected. In the flat portions of the country they consisted usually of an earthen cone raised upon a circular foundation of masonry, with one or more chambers within for the reception of the dead. The largest of these tumuli was that called the Cucumella, at Vulci.

In the mountains, where material was abundant, it was customary to bury the dead in a square stone chamber, surmounted by a pyramidal roof, and entered by a doorway ornamented with the Greek architrave. There are several examples of these at Castel d'Asso.

A third form of sepulchre was the hypogee, or underground tomb, the entrance to which was marked by a colonnade of the Tuscan order, carved in the face of the rock; the interior apartment being usually rectangular, and reached by a staircase. The walls were decorated with paintings, and the tomb filled with vases, tripods, arms, and other votive offerings. The body was generally either placed in a stone sarcophagus or laid upon a bronze bed. The ceilings in the older tombs were either flat, being cut in the natural rock, with piers left as supports, and ornamented with sunken panels, or constructed of inclined slabs, resting against and sustaining each other.

The corbelled vaults, similar to those of Mycenæ, were employed for a considerable number of these buildings, but were subsequently relinquished for vaults of voussoirs, or wedge-shaped stones. The invention of the semicircular vault, the joints of which converge to a common centre, was long attributed to the Etruscans, but we have seen that recent discoveries have shown that it was already in use in Egypt and Assyria many centuries before.

This principle, however, was the chief feature of Etruscan architecture, and its great legacy to succeeding styles.

Etruria as well as Greece sent artists to Rome, and the conjunction of the methods used in the two countries produced Roman art.

"The Romans took from the Etruscans the semicircular arch, formed of jointed stones; from the populations of the Campagna they obtained the general arrangement of sacred edifices, the Greek orders, the distribution and decoration of private dwellings. They drew thus from two different sources, and endeavoured to unite two principles diametrically opposed to one another—the principle of the Greek lintel and the Etruscan arch. In doing this they show clearly that their ideas upon the arts were but little better than those of pirates, whose acts are actuated by pride rather than by taste, and who adorn themselves in spoils of dis-

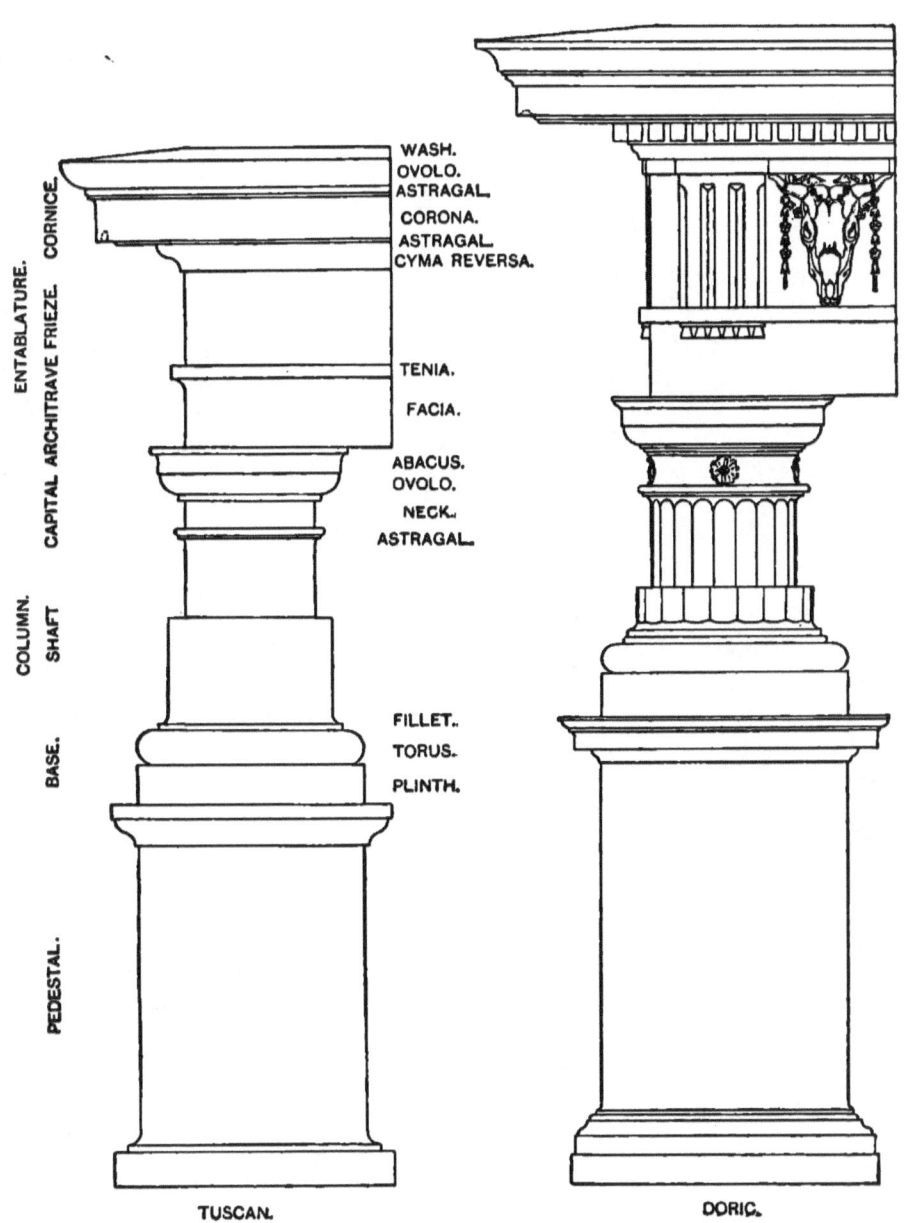

THE ROMAN ORDERS.

IONIC.

COMPOSITE.

tinctly different origin, the mingling of which produces unseemly contrasts." *

In fact, the Greek orders, modified to suit the taste of the Romans, and combined with the Etruscan arch and vault, formed the basis of all Roman architecture. The scale of their buildings, however, was vastly greater than that of those upon which they were modelled. The colonnades of their palaces and the arcades of their aqueducts were to be measured by the mile, the vaults of their baths were of prodigious span, and, in general size and number, the edifices erected by the Romans exceeded anything which had come before them.

The Roman orders were five in number, namely, the Tuscan, Doric, Ionic, Corinthian, and Composite.

The Tuscan we have already examined. The Doric was somewhat more elaborate, having additional mouldings in the capital and base, and the triglyph ornament in the frieze. The Ionic and Corinthian were but modifications of the corresponding Greek orders. The Composite was of the same proportion as the Corinthian, the capital being a combination of the Ionic and Corinthian.

The Corinthian order was the most generally used, its rich character suiting the ostentatious ideas of the Romans. The superposition of columns was a common method of indicating different stories, and

---

* Entretiens sur l'Architecture.

different orders were often employed where different-sized columns occurred in the same building.

In plan the Roman buildings were rectangular, polygonal, and circular, or combinations of these geometrical forms. The materials used were local stone, imported marbles and alabaster, and bricks, which were flatter and longer than the form employed at the present day. The Romans excelled in their mortars and cements, which were of a strength sufficient to make their walls virtually of one mass.

In bonding their stone they employed various methods, including those of the Greeks. Of these, a favourite one was the building of exterior faces only, and filling up the intervening space with broken stone and mortar. In order to produce the greatest effect at the least cost, in the use of marble, they resorted to panelling the external surfaces only with thin slabs. Interiors were lined with stucco and frequently ornamented with paintings, and the floors inlaid with mosaic. Roman mouldings were sections of the sphere, differing from the Greek, which were hyperbolas or parabolas.

The chief constructions of the Romans were houses, temples, palaces, amphitheatres, theatres, aqueducts, sewers, baths, triumphal arches, tombs and commemorative structures, camps, bridges, and basilicas.

In, and in close proximity to, the Forum Romanum, or Campo Vaccino, are admirable examples of nearly all these different buildings. The level of the

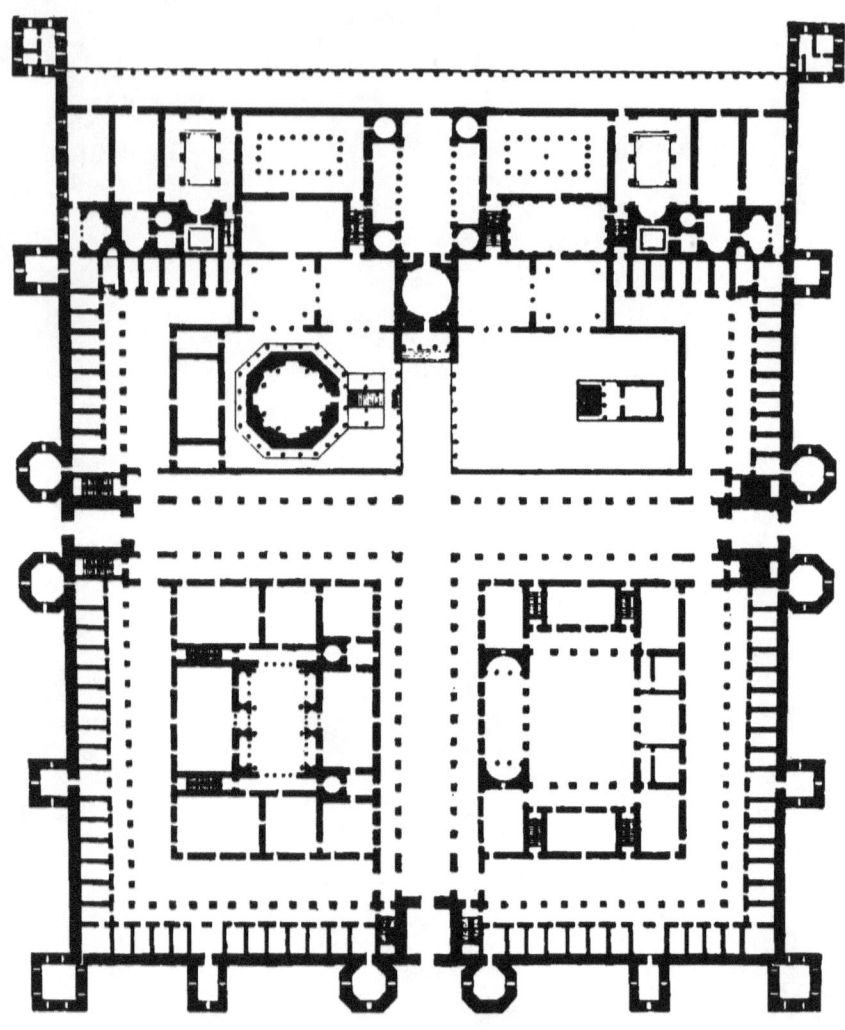

PALACE OF DIOCLETIAN AT SPALATRO.

(From Durand.)

ancient market-place is several feet below that of the streets of modern Rome, but in the excavated portions are to be seen the old pavements of irregular stone slabs, laid upon concrete foundations and worn with the wheels of chariots.

Many ruined temples, the arches of Septimius Severus, of Titus and Constantine, the palace of the Cæsars, the Colosseum, and the Baths of Constantine are collected here within a stone's throw. By taking up each class of buildings separately, however, we will get a better idea of the nature of Roman architecture than by a description of isolated buildings.

Roman houses resembled in a measure the Greek, the different apartments being grouped around inner courts. The rooms consisted of halls, vestibules, banqueting-rooms, and sleeping-chambers, the women not being separated from the men, as was the case in Greece. The courts were surrounded by colonnades and in the centre a well was usually placed, to receive the water from the roofs. Many of the houses were several stories in height, but a limit to their altitude was fixed by decree.

The excavations in Pompeii have uncovered many interesting specimens of private dwellings, richly decorated with several paintings and having elaborate mosaic patterns on their floors.

In the city of Rome the palace of the Cæsars was the most notable example of domestic architecture, but at the present day it is difficult to discern among the débris and fallen walls what its original plan may have been. Some paintings in the so-called house of Livia, upon the plateau of the palace, however, show that the artists of the period had attained a high degree of merit.

Roman temples consisted generally of a cella or rectangular apartment, preceded by a porch, the whole being raised on a platform, reached by stairs and enclosed by a colonnade below. Occasionally there was a double cella, with separate entrances and porches, as in that of Venus and Rome; and there are two remaining examples of circular temples—that of Vesta, on the Tiber, in Rome, and of the Sybil, at Tivoli—while still another type, that of the Pantheon of Agrippa, had a circular cella and a rectangular porch.

The Corinthian order was the most frequently employed, that of the temple of Jupiter Stator being the richest, while those of the Pantheon, the Maison Carrée, at Nîmes, and of the temple of Antonine and Faustina are admirable specimens.

This last is one of the best-preserved temples, being very nearly entire at the present time; its frieze is of the most refined workmanship, representing allegorical animals, plants, etc.

The temple of Fortuna Virilis is a good example of the Ionic order, but this order was never a favourite with the Romans.

A debased form of Ionic is that of the temple of Concord, or Vespasian, where the capital is altered

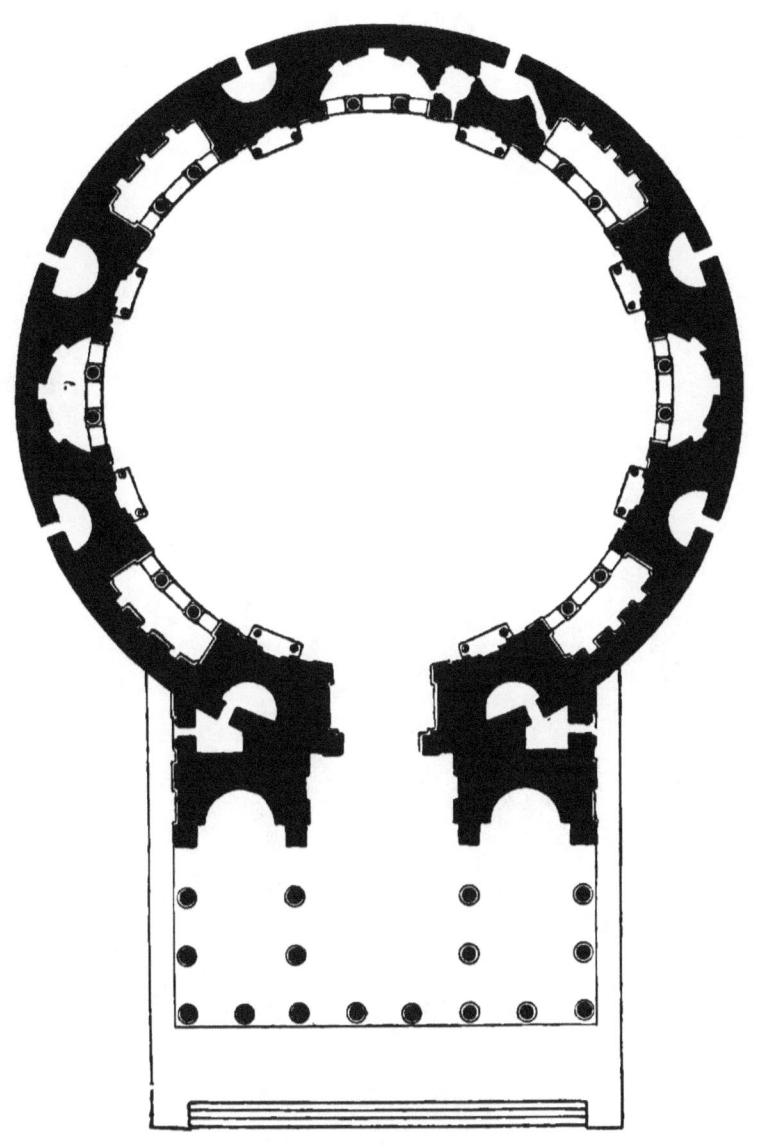

PLAN OF THE PANTHEON AT ROME.

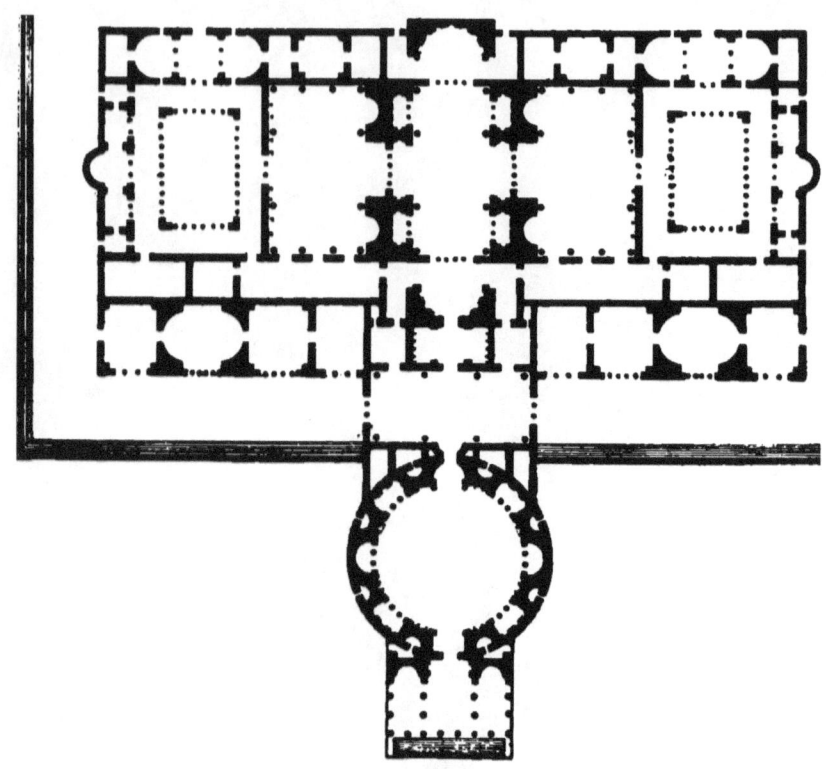

PLAN OF THE BATHS OF AGRIPPA CONNECTING WITH THE PANTHEON, ACCORDING TO P

(*From Durand.*)

to a considerable extent and a rope moulding added. A remarkable constructional feature of this temple is the relieving arch of brick, concealed behind the frieze, to diminish the weight on the lintel below.

The great drum of the Pantheon, enclosed by a circular vault, is one of the earliest examples of domical architecture. A notable feature in it is the absence of the keystone, which is replaced here by an open ring, leaving an aperture for the entrance of light. The walls are pierced with niches and relieved by immense arches. The pediment of the porch is one of the most perfect remaining; in height its proportion exceeds that of Greek temples.

The temple of Diana, at Nîmes, is a remarkable structure, having three aisles, the central one being decorated with niches and columns, which support an entablature and a ribbed vault.

The ruined temples of Baalbek and of Jupiter Olympius, at Athens, are among the most colossal of this class of building. The Corinthian columns of the latter measure upward of sixty feet, and their capitals are of singularly fine workmanship.

The Emperor Hadrian embellished Athens with numerous and splendid buildings, which to-day have assumed the colour and ruined appearance of the older constructions of the time of Pericles.

Of the temple of Jupiter Olympius there are scarcely more than a dozen columns standing of the original one hundred and twenty. The Turks ground up many of them to make lime for their mortar.

The Romans took their conception of the theatre from the Greeks. The building was composed of two parts, the one devoted to the stage and its accessories, and the other to the accommodation of the audience. The stage was usually in the form of a rectangle, the longer side of which formed the diameter of the semicircle, which was the plan of the second part. The latter was composed of concentric seats in successive steps, to which access was had by stairs radiating from the centre and leading to an upper surrounding gallery. At the foot of these steps a space was reserved called the orchestra (Greek, "dancing place"), usually occupied by the senators. The stage, which was decorated with columns and niches, was raised above the orchestra, and was connected with the actors' rooms. The wall at the back of the stage was carried up to the level of the circular enclosing wall, and treated with superposed orders. The theatre of Marcellus, in Rome, and those of Herculaneum, Arles, and Orange are among the best examples.

The most celebrated amphitheatre (amphi theatron, Greek, "double theatre") is that commonly known as the Colosseum, or Flavian Amphitheatre. It is composed of the arena or oval space, occupied by the combatants, and of the "visorium," formed by concentric seats placed in tiers, one above the other.

It was capable of seating eighty thousand spec-

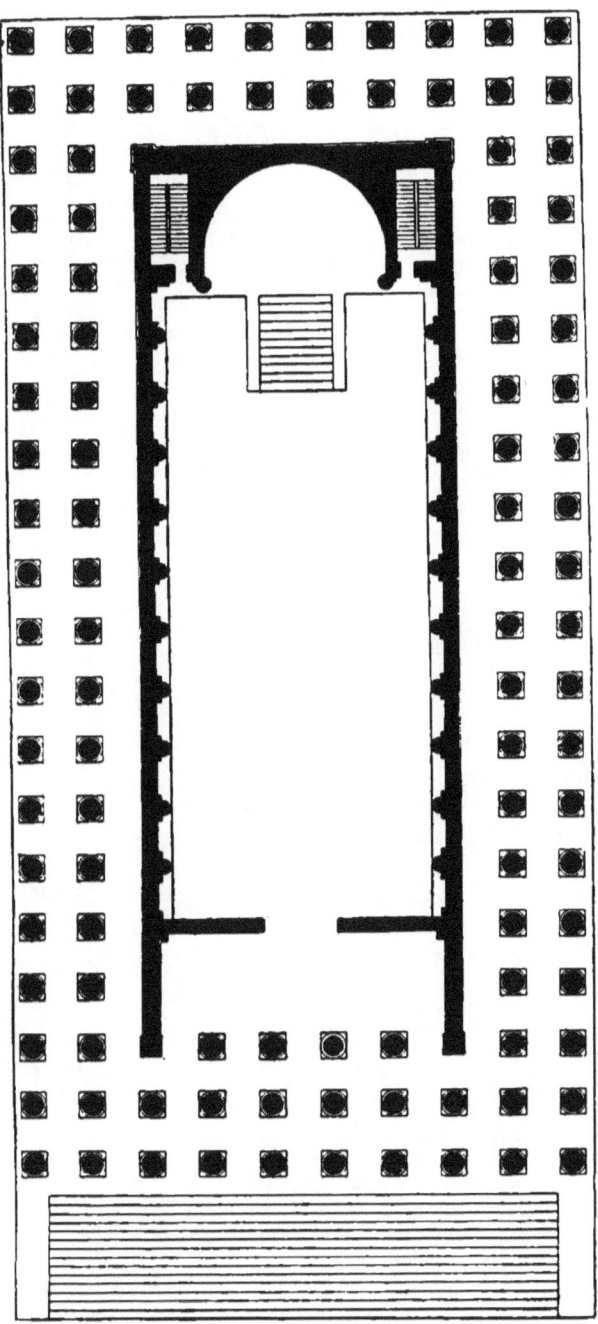

PLAN OF THE TEMPLE OF THE SUN AT BAALBEK.

tators, and upon its arena four thousand gladiators have fought at a time. It was here that before commencing their combats they came to the foot of the emperor's throne, saluting him with the celebrated cry, " Morituri te salutamus."

The substructure of the building consists of vaulted passages, communicating with the visorium by numerous staircases, and with the exterior by the doors called "vomitoria." The arena was surrounded by a ditch of running water, and under it were chambers in which prisoners and animals were confined.

The visorium was divided according to the rank of its occupants. The upper classes occupied the "podium" or lower gallery, which extended on either side of the emperor's throne, at the extremity of the longer axis of the building. For protection from the elements during performances an immense sail was stretched over the building from posts inserted in stone brackets at the top of the exterior wall.

The heights of the three lower stories of the Colosseum are marked externally by arcades and superposed orders with engaged columns, Doric, Ionic, and Corinthian, and the fourth and upper one by Corinthian pilasters. The entablatures of each order are carried around the entire circumference of the building.

Architects generally criticise this construction adversely, for " if, on the one hand, the engaged columns might be supposed to serve as buttresses and thus become a useful decoration, it must be admitted, on the other, that the projecting entablatures carried from column to column do more harm than good as regards the solidity of the building. [The architrave having no longer the force of the Greek lintel, being composed of several blocks supported by the arch below.] The Romans, however, did not always falsely apply the true principles of architecture. In the arena of Nîmes, for instance, the two superposed orders which serve as buttresses between the arcades of the two stories on the exterior of that building, are real buttresses. The lower order is composed of projecting piers, the upper order of engaged columns; the cornices follow the contour of each pilaster or column and do not form those projecting belts which are placed so clumsily and uselessly around such buildings as the theatre of Marcellus and the Colosseum of Rome." *

This amphitheatre was commenced by Vespasian and continued under Titus, who dedicated it in the year 80 A. D. In the ninth century it was half destroyed, and subsequently became a quarry, from which materials were extracted for the construction of the Farnese palace and other buildings.

A large part, however, is standing to-day, having been rescued from total destruction by order of Pope Benoit XIV.

There are celebrated remains of amphitheatres at Verona, Pola, Capua, Arles, and Nimes.

---

* Viollet le Duc.

Circuses and Naumachias belong to the same class of buildings, the one serving for chariot and other races, and the other for naval combats. The arena in each was oval in plan and from it rose the successive tiers of broad steps upon which the seats were ranged. At the top a portico decorated with statues enclosed the whole building.

The Circus Maximus was the most important of these, containing numerous splendid statues and obelisks, and covering a vast area.

The aqueducts of ancient Rome stretched for miles across the Campagna. The channel in which the water flowed was supported by one or more arcades, superposed according to the height required. These arcades consisted of round brick arches carried on substantial piers, and were placed where possible upon the highest elevations of the country they traversed. At intervals wide basins were provided for the collection of sediment, and reservoirs received the water at their termination. From the latter pipes supplied the baths and private dwellings.

In France the famous Pont du Gard is a portion of an immense Roman aqueduct formed of three rows of arcades, which supplied the city of Nîmes.

Bridges were constructed on the same principle; the arches increasing their span according to the depth of the piers upon which they rested, being generally of two stories, the upper one having double the number of piers.

The Roman bridges and aqueducts in Spain are

among the most justly celebrated, notably those of Segovia, Tarragona, and Alcantara. Bridging rivers by boats was a common method in use by the Roman armies under Julius Cæsar. We have also an account of a wooden bridge over the Danube, constructed by Trajan.

Under every street in Rome there ran vaulted sewers conducting all impurities into the main artery, called the Cloaca Maxima, which in turn discharged its contents into the Tiber. This sewer is one of the oldest examples of the use of voussoirs, dating from the reign of Tarquinius Priscus. It is covered by a triple vault, sustaining the street above.

Agrippa conducted the waters of several streams into the sewers and appointed inspectors to keep them in repair and good order.

In the building of the baths of Rome, Agrippa, Nero, Vespasian, Caracalla, Titus, Diocletian, and Constantine vied with each other in the production of the most magnificent structures. They are to-day in a hopelessly ruined condition, but from the numerous fragments of carved marble and panelled stucco lying on their sites, and from the rich paintings and mosaics of the baths of Titus and Caracalla, it is not difficult to form an idea of their original splendour.

It is not a little significant of what their rich decoration must have been to note that such marvels of statuary as the Laocoon, the Farnese Bull, and the Gladiators have been discovered within them.

Besides the necessary administrative rooms, these buildings generally contained a frigidarium or cold bath, a tepidarium or warm bath, and a sudatorium, circular in form and covered in by a dome. The walls, built of brick, were pierced with niches and supported high cross and barrel vaults of immense span. It has been conjectured that the Pantheon was the entrance hall of the baths of Agrippa, the porch having been added at a later period when the building was converted into a temple.

The chief commemorative structures were triumphal arches and votive columns. The former were of two kinds, having either one main arched opening, or a large central arch for vehicles and two lower ones on either side for foot passengers. The arch of Titus in Rome is an example of the first, its main arch being flanked by composite columns, supporting a richly carved entablature, which is in turn surmounted by an attic, inscribed with the dedication to the conqueror by the Senate and Roman people. The bassi relievi employed in its decoration represent the sacking of Jerusalem by Titus; a specially notable feature among the spoils depicted being the golden candelabra with the seven sockets, mentioned in Scripture history.

The arches of Constantine and Septimius Severus are of the second category. They are covered with rich sculpture and are of very beautiful proportion. Famous arches are those of Orange in the south of France, Beneventum, Ancona, Rimini,

Pola, and Athens. Everywhere, in fact, where a victory was to be commemorated, or the termination of a great military road to be marked, it was customary to erect an arch.

Another method of paying homage to great men was to erect columns surmounted by their statues. The columns of Trajan and Antoninus in Rome are especially remarkable. The former is the higher and of the best workmanship. The pedestal upon which it rests is ornamented with elaborate carvings representing the arms of conquered nations, and is enriched at the four upper corners of its cornice by imperial eagles with garlands suspended between them. A wreath replaces the torus or round mould at the base of the column, and around the shaft is wound a ribbon of sculpture, representing a triumphal procession, which terminates at the capital. Isolated columns were also often employed for the inscription of legal notices, as boundary-marks, or for marking military limits.

The gates at the entrances of the principal cities were similar to the triumphal arches. There are two especially fine examples in France, those of Autun and Treves. In these the attic story is replaced by a gallery connecting the two flanking wings, which are several stories in height, and contain chambers which it is commonly supposed were used as courts of justice.

Roman camps were regulated and arranged with

military precision, and were of two descriptions. The one, erected for temporary use, was defended by a rude palisade of branches and a ditch, the other, the "castra hiberna," or winter quarters, was generally a permanent structure, built of brick, containing within a square enclosure the barracks, workshops, hospitals, and other necessary buildings. This enclosure was divided by cross-roads, passing through gates in the outer wall. The gate facing the enemy was called the porta prætoria, hence prætorian camp.

Necrological monuments were built in various forms, from the simple tablet to the immense mausoleums of the emperors. Just without the walls of Rome are still to be seen the remains of the sepulchre of Caius Sestius, a large pyramid containing a chamber several feet above the ground level. Farther out, on the Appian Way, is the tomb of Cæcilia Metella, a cylindrical structure upon a square base, of considerable magnitude. The exterior is simple, the only decoration being a series of ox-skulls in the frieze. This building was probably originally surmounted by an earthen cone, after the manner of the Etruscan tombs.

The tomb of Augustus was constructed in a similar manner but on a larger scale. The entrance was preceded by a porch and the exterior walls contained niches. The conical mound above was planted with trees and shrubbery.

The Scipios were buried in stone sarcophagi in a

subterranean chamber, which has been but recently discovered.

A curious monument was that of the Horatii, consisting of a rectangular block of masonry, containing the sepulchre, surmounted by four stone cones, grouped around a fifth and higher one. These probably had a symbolical meaning, as a similar structure, called the tomb of Porsenna, is said to have existed in Etruria.

By far the most magnificent building of the kind was the Mausoleum, or Mole of Hadrian, the ruins of which now go by the name of the Castel St. Angelo. The tomb rose conspicuously on the banks above the Tiber, on a square foundation; its two upper stories were circular in plan, and decorated with colonnades and statuary, and the whole was capped by an immense roof, terminated by a pineapple of bronze.

The tombs of St. Helena and St. Costanza were circular structures similar to that of Cæcilia Metella, the cone of earth, however, being replaced by a dome. The interior of the tomb of St. Costanza was divided by columns which sustained a vault connecting with the outer wall.

The practice of burning bodies and preserving their ashes gave rise also to the building of columbariums, rectangular structures containing in their walls receptacles for funereal urns.

In the valley of Jerusalem the hypogee was the form of sepulchre commonly adopted, its entrance being decorated with a colonnade of one of the Roman orders.

Basilicas were the law courts of the Roman people and places of assembly for the transaction of their daily affairs. On the exterior, these buildings were surrounded by numerous courts and porticos, where the merchants assembled daily to discuss their affairs or to await the result of the trials conducted within. In the interior they contained a large hall or nave flanked by side aisles, preceding a transept or further room which was terminated by a semicircular apse. This apse was occupied by the magistrate while presiding in the cases submitted to his decision.

The ruins of the basilicas of Titus and Maxentius remain, at the present day, in sufficient preservation to show that in the one a flat ceiling of timber was employed, and in the other a system of intersecting vaults similar in construction to those of the baths of Caracalla. There are traces of several ancient buildings of this kind, but it is supposed that many were pulled down by the Christians, who erected churches on their sites, using the old basilica as their model.

The plan was, in reality, but an improvement on that of the Roman temple, the side aisles and transepts being naturally developed additions to the older cella to which the apse had been added previously in many examples.

The great administrative power governing the

erection of the buildings of Rome was one of the most remarkable features connected with them. Architecture with the Romans was a means to an end, this end being the construction of edifices suiting their requirements and their desire for display. No scope was allowed for individual talent or ingenuity, unless employed in the carrying out of a distinct programme, laid down by those in power; each building forming part of a great scheme, prevailing throughout the conquered world.

In Greece architectural works were produced in the different cities and states under the guidance of independent artists, with the co-operation of their fellow-citizens who were eager to attain the true principles of art; in Rome and the Roman world, art was entirely subservient to a system of politics which ran through all departments.

The vast wealth which flowed into the capital from tributary provinces was the great mainstay which permitted the execution of so many vast and expensive structures, forming a collection never surpassed. Roman art corresponded with the national character, for it was coarse and ostentatious, but at the same time vast and strong. The population of Athens delighted in intellectual pursuits, in philosophy, in art; it crowded the seats on the slope of the Acropolis to enjoy the wit and satire of Æschylus and Sophocles, and the palæstra to witness the development of bodily grace and dexterity, while the Romans flocked to the Colosseum for the enjoyment of scenes of blood and carnage, to gaze upon the slaughter of captives and the anguish of animals. The force of their government, nevertheless, was unquestionable; their patriotism, unlike that of the Greeks, was unaffected by civic jealousies or party feeling; they trod rough-shod upon the nations, but they planted everywhere the imprint of their heroic civilization and made their capital the centre of the world, and left to it, for all ages, the proud appellation of the Eternal City.

VI.

THE EARLY CHRISTIAN STYLE.

AFTER the conversion of the Emperor Constantine to Christianity, in the fourth century, the Christians who, as a persecuted sect had hitherto held their religious observances in hiding, in the catacombs of Rome, adopted the basilica as the most convenient form of building for the purposes of their worship. The bishop occupied a throne in the apse, surrounded by the presbyters or fathers of the church, and the congregation of the faithful filled the central nave.

For several centuries this plan was but little changed, the only notable additions to it being the continuation of the transept beyond the line of the walls of the nave, thus making it cruciform; the occasional substitution of double aisles, making five divisions in the body of the church, instead of the original three, and the addition of a tower or belfry.

All subsequent churches, whether Romanesque, Gothic, or Renaissance were constructed on but slight modifications of this original plan, which, in fact, was itself evolved from that of the Roman temple.

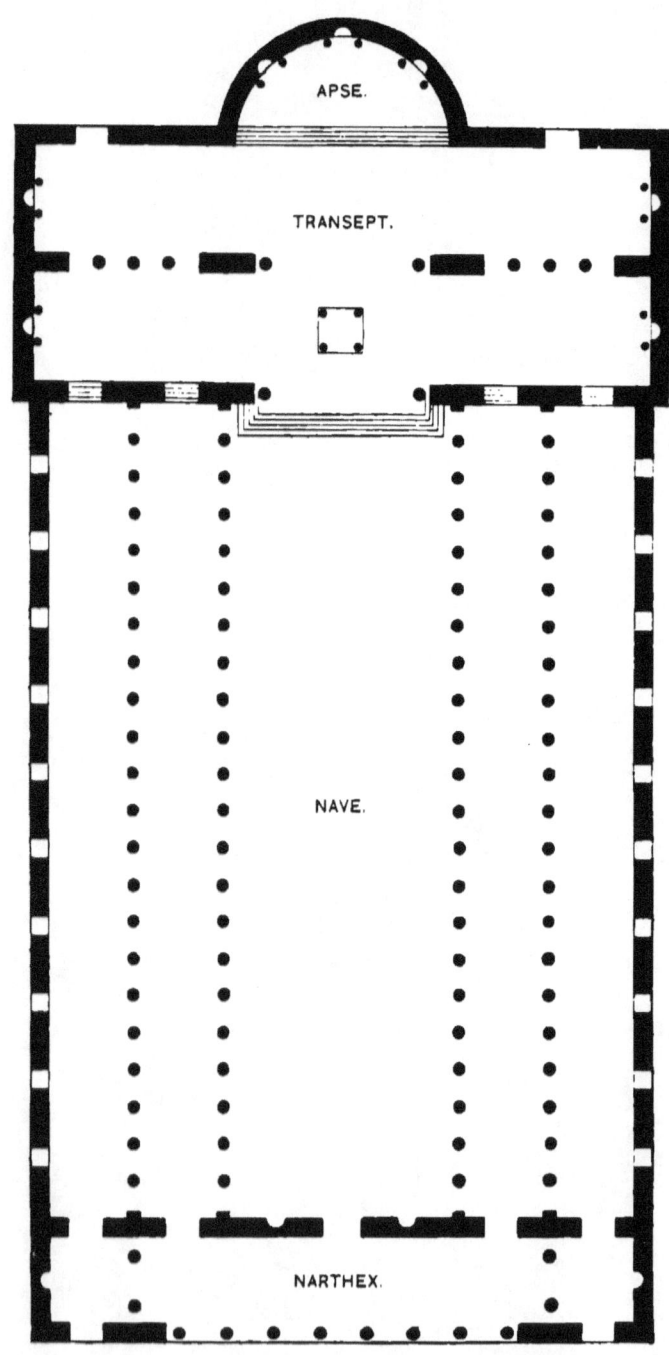

PLAN OF THE OLD BASILICA OF ST PAUL'S BEYOND THE WALLS.

The first basilicas erected for Christian worship had double aisles; this form was, however, soon discontinued, probably owing to the difficulty of observing the offices of the clergy from the outer aisle. Of these St. Peter's, St. Paul's beyond the walls, and St. John Lateran were the finest examples. The first-named was built upon the site of the present cathedral, and was removed in the sixteenth century to make room for it. Its dimensions were of notable size, being about 380 feet long by 212 feet in width. It was preceded by an atrium, or open court, surrounded by a colonnade, in which the Christians met to transact their affairs. The basilica of St. Paul's was destroyed by fire in the early part of this century, and a new structure resembling the old was erected in its place on a scale of great magnificence. The columns of its Corinthian colonnade and the floor are of polished marble and the wooden roof lavishly ornamented with carving and gilding. The transept is enriched with mosaics, and contains a baldachin over the altar, in which malachite and other choice stones have been used unsparingly.

A typical basilica was generally arranged as follows: The atrium or quadrangular open court, surrounded by porticos, preceded the main building, or was replaced by a porch composed of columns sustaining a low roof which was called the narthex. Within, the structure was divided into a nave, side aisles, transept, and apse. The nave (derived from "navis," a vessel, symbolical of that of St. Peter) was loftier than the adjoining aisles, the upper wall being usually panelled with pictures and pierced at the top by a range of windows, from which the Gothic clerestory was derived later on. In one or two instances where the side aisles had a second story or upper gallery for the women, the panels and windows were placed in the outer wall.

The interior lines of columns were usually of the Ionic or Corinthian orders, having been taken from older buildings, but if new they were of stouter proportions than the Classical models. These columns supported either a continuous architrave or circular arches.

Wooden doors, often covered by chased bronze, were hung in the main entrance and the wall above was usually pierced by a round window or bull's-eye, afterward developed into the rose window. At the other end of the nave a wide arched opening, called the triumphal arch, connected it with the transept.

An enclosure, separated from the body of the church by a balustrade, at the upper end of the nave, contained the seats of the choristers and the reading-desks.

The altar was placed in the transept and was frequently surmounted by a baldachin composed of four or six columns supporting a light dome. Behind the altar in the centre of the apse was the throne (cathedra) occupied by the bishop (episcopus), being raised by steps from the semicircular stone seats (exedra) used by the presbyters, which were covered with carpets. The walls of the transept and apse were inlaid with mosaic inscriptions and pictures, in which the head of our Saviour, the figures of saints and holy emblems were the chief subjects. Deep blue, purple, and green were the prevailing colours and the letters were of gold. The floors were decorated with mosaic patterns. The roofs were either flat with sunken panels framed with mouldings and gilded ornaments, or else showed the open trussed wood-work, though the latter was the exception. Externally there was no attempt at enrichment, the exterior generally offering a great contrast to the lavish internal decorations.

At the present day nearly all the basilicas have undergone transformation, the old roofs have been replaced, the walls covered with a modern adornment of pilasters and gaudy paintings, the colonnades have been broken through to allow of entrances to side-chapels, or disfigured by the heterogeneous decoration of the eighteenth century, and the exteriors treated with renaissance façades.

Nevertheless the general plan and arrangements have remained substantially the same, and we have very interesting specimens of this class of building in St. Maria Maggiore, St. Agnese, San Clemente, and others, in Rome, San Appolinare, in Ravenna, the basilicas at Torcello, in the Venetian lagoons, and later examples in St. Ambrogio, of Milan, and St. Maria Sopra Minerva, in Rome.

The basilica at Torcello was built mainly from fragments of an older church upon the mainland at Altino. The bishop's throne is one of the most interesting and best preserved examples we have.

The Greek name for this, cathedra, was the origin of our term cathedral, applied to churches containing the bishop's seat, there being no architectural distinction between the buildings.

From the tombs of the Romans the Christians derived their conception of the edifices which they used as baptisteries. Their exterior walls were either polygonal or circular, and of severe simplicity. The interiors were generally divided by a row of columns sustaining a round vault, and forming a circular enclosure in which the font was placed. A wall, carried on these columns, contained windows, and served as a lantern to light the building. This wall occasionally supported a dome. San Stephano Rotondo, in Rome; St. Angeli, in Perugia, and St. Vitale, in Ravenna, are the best examples among the many found in Italy.

San Stephano has a double range of interior columns, taken from Roman temples, the one supporting an entablature, and the other a series of arches. The church has been much modified by successive alterations, and the interior is ornamented with curious paintings, representing the sufferings of the martyrs.

The baptistery of St. Angeli is smaller, but has preserved its original form in a greater degree.

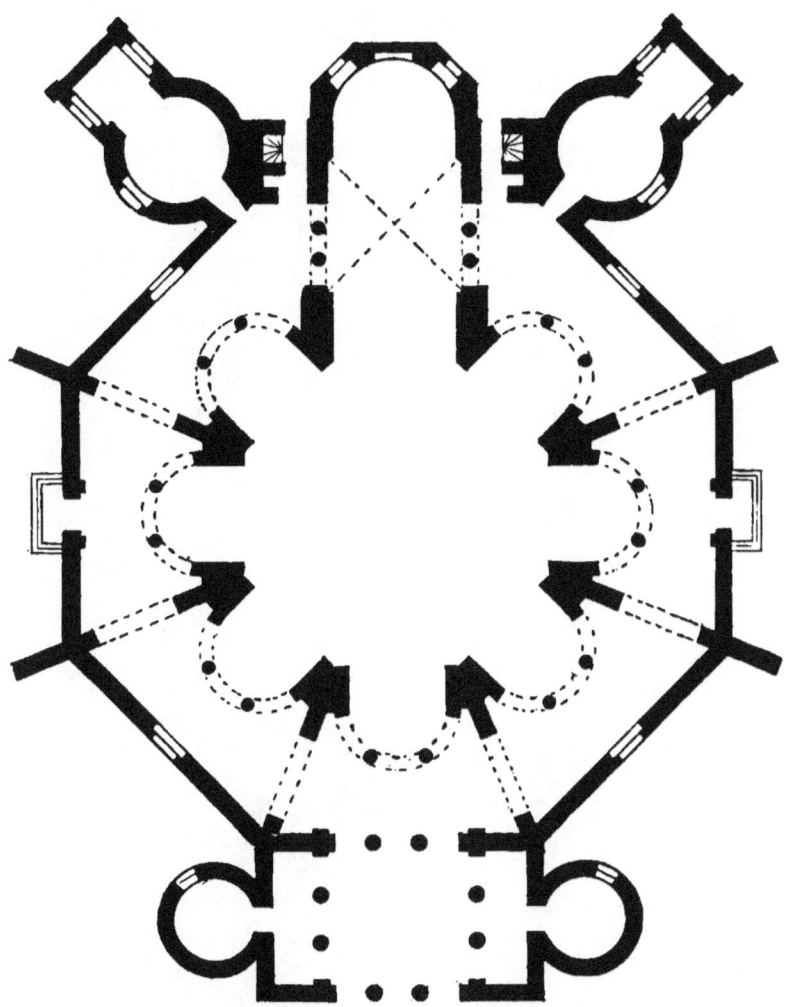

ST. VITALE, OF RAVENNA.

THE TEMPLE OF MINERVA MEDICA.

St. Vitale is a type of structure much copied in subsequent buildings. It is itself modelled on the so-called temple of Minerva Medica, differing only in having an octagon instead of a decagon plan. Of this Fergusson gives the following account:

" It certainly belongs to the best days of the Roman empire, if, indeed, it be not a Christian building, which I am very much inclined to believe it is, for on comparing it with the baptistery of Constantine and the tomb of St. Contanza, it shows a considerable advance in construction on both of these buildings, and a greater similarity to San Vitale, at Ravenna, and other buildings of that time, than to anything else now found in Rome.

It has a dome eighty feet in diameter, resting on a decagon of singularly light and elegant construction. Nine of the compartments contain niches, which give great room on the floor, as well as variety and lightness to the general design. Above this is a clerestory of ten well-proportioned windows, which give light to the building; perhaps not in so effective a manner as the one eye of the Pantheon, though by a far more convenient arrangement, to protect from the elements a people who did not possess glass.

" So far as I know, all domed buildings erected by the Romans up to the time of Constantine, and, indeed, long afterward, were circular in the interior, though they were sometimes octagonal externally. This, however, is a polygon both internally and on the outside, and the mode in which the dome is placed on the polygon shows the first rudiments of the pendentive system, which was afterward carried to such perfection by the Byzantine architects, but is nowhere else to be found in Rome. It probably was for the purpose of somewhat diminishing the difficulties of this construction that the architect adopted a figure with ten instead of eight sides."

The plans of the temple of Vesta and of the baptistery of Constantine have been placed here next to one another in order to show the transposition of the columns from the exterior to the interior, which is the chief distinction between the Roman circular buildings and Christian baptisteries.

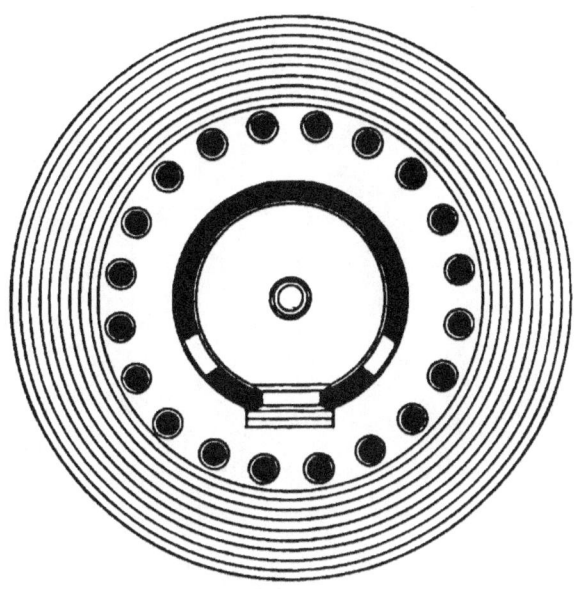

THE TEMPLE OF VESTA, SOMETIMES CALLED THE TEMPLE OF HERCULES.

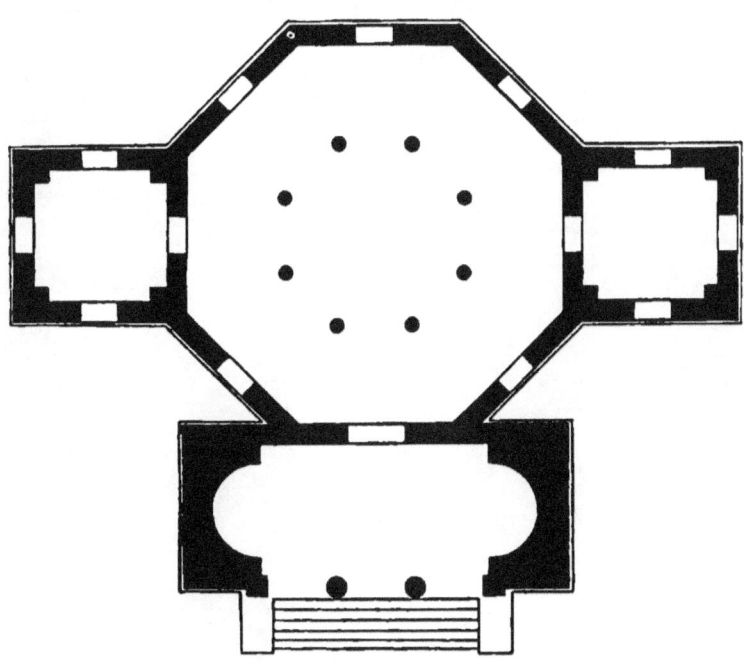

THE BAPTISTERY OF CONSTANTINE.

VII.

THE BYZANTINE STYLE.

CONSTANTINE and his mother St. Helena built churches in Bethlehem, Jerusalem, and Antioch, and embellished Constantinople with numerous splendid edifices. The Eastern basilicas preserved the same character in their construction as those of Italy, but their component parts were more homogeneous, the materials being specially prepared, instead of being borrowed from ancient buildings. The first vigour of emancipated Christianity found vent not only in the erection of edifices devoted to its religious observances, but in the infliction of irreparable injury upon the pagan monuments of Greece and Rome. Constantine brought many fragments of these Classical buildings to the new capital, but they have been destroyed, together with the palaces, churches, and baths which he built there, in successive invasions, by fire, or by earthquakes.

In Thessalonica there are two good examples of early basilicas—the old mosque and the five-aisled church of St. Demetrius; and in Northern Syria there are many admirable specimens. Of these the churches at Rouheilia, Kalb-Louzeh, and Tourmanim deserve special mention.

The latter is a particularly successful building, designed in the new style growing out of the older Roman one, and is a model structure, being constructed exactly in accordance with the requirements of the early Church.

In plan, the Syrian conventual buildings depart but slightly from that of the basilicas of Rome, but in their interior treatment they show a gradual secession from the rules which govern Classical buildings, retaining only their useful and discarding their merely ornamental features.

When the seat of the empire had been transferred to Byzance, the Christians carried with them the principles of the arch and the vault and combined them in a new form of structure. This construction, differing from that employed in Rome, combined with Eastern or late Greek forms of ornament, produced a new style called the Byzantine.

The distinctive feature of this method of construction was the placing of the circular dome, not upon a cylindrical drum, as had been done by the Romans in the Pantheon and other buildings, but upon four walls, square in plan, surmounted by semicircular arches, with the intervening spaces occupied by pendentives. To each side of this central square was joined a nave of the same length, forming thus in plan a Greek cross, that is, one having each arm equally long. These naves were

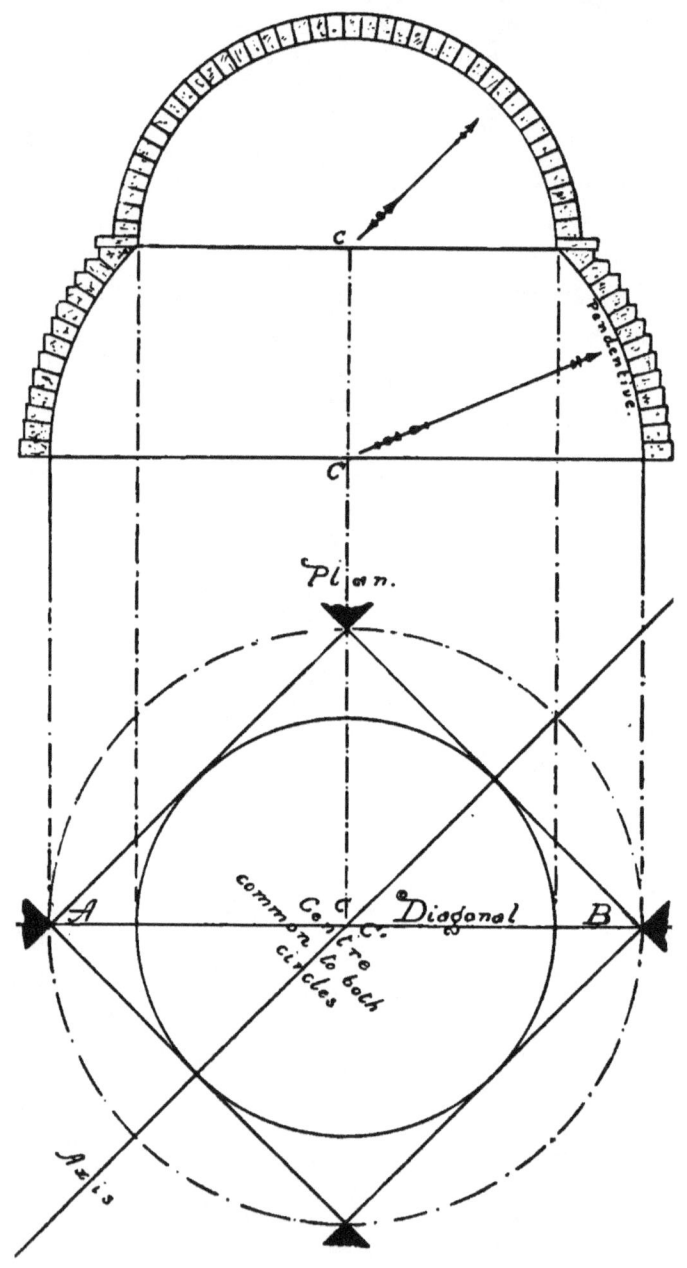

THE PENDENTIVE SYSTEM IN BYZANTINE DOMES.

usually short, more frequently semicircular than rectangular, and often terminated by an apse.

We have seen, in the baptistery of St. Vitale, at Ravenna (in which Greek artists were undoubtedly employed), a tendency to reduce the number of sides of polygonal buildings supporting circular domes; the architects of Byzance were therefore merely taking another step in the same direction when they placed the dome upon a quadrilateral substructure.

To comprehend the pendentive, let us take a circle and inscribe within it a square; at the four angles of the square we will place solid piers of masonry and connect them with semicircular arches. Let us now suppose that a hemispherical dome had been built upon this circle as plan, and we will see that the planes of the arches and the plane passing at the level of the top of the keystones of the arches, in intersecting this dome, would leave but four triangular portions of it. These triangular portions are called pendentives, and are the only portions of the original hemisphere which are actually built. As this hemisphere would have been necessarily constructed of materials the joints of which would have radiated from the centre of the sphere, so also do the joints of the pendentives radiate from this same centre, which is identical with the centre of the original circle. The plane passing at the level of the top of the keystones in intersecting the hemisphere describes another circle, upon which the actual dome is placed.

The question has not been established satisfactorily whether the Byzantine architects really understood the pendentive, as in many instances they resorted to less scientific methods of filling in the vacant spaces between the arches and the upper dome, but the only logical method of constructing it is that which has just been described.

In building domes, it was not uncommon in the East to replace stone-work by light terra cotta pipes, fitting into each other, giving great lightness and comparative strength.

Justinian gave a marked impetus to architectural work and to the building of religious edifices in particular. He commissioned Anthemius of Thralles, and Isidor of Miletus, to execute the plans for the new church of St. Sophia, upon the site of an older building of Constantine, also dedicated to the "Holy Wisdom," which had been burnt during an emeute soon after it had been repaired by Theodosius.

Justinian had already built the church of Sergius and Bacchus in Constantinople, on a plan nearly identical with that of St. Vitale, at Ravenna, with the exception that the whole structure was externally in the form of a square, enclosing the octagon supporting the dome. This served as a stepping-stone to the conception of the larger church, which became the type of all subsequent Byzantine constructions.

By comparing the plans of the Pantheon, the temple of Minerva Medica, the baptistery of Con-

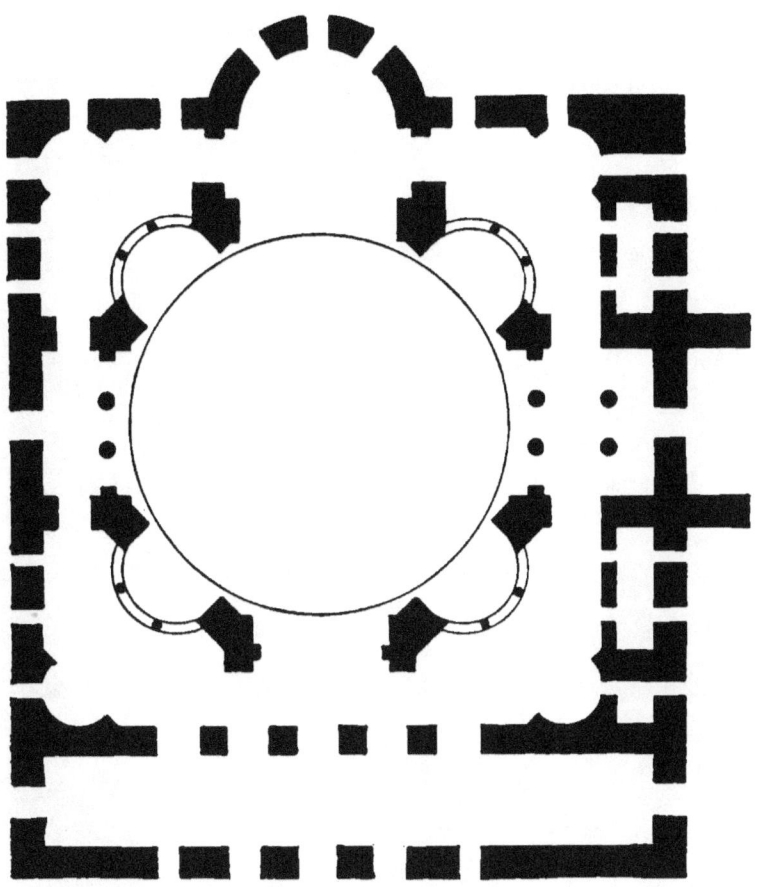

CHURCH OF SERGIUS AND BACCHUS AT CONSTANTINOPLE.

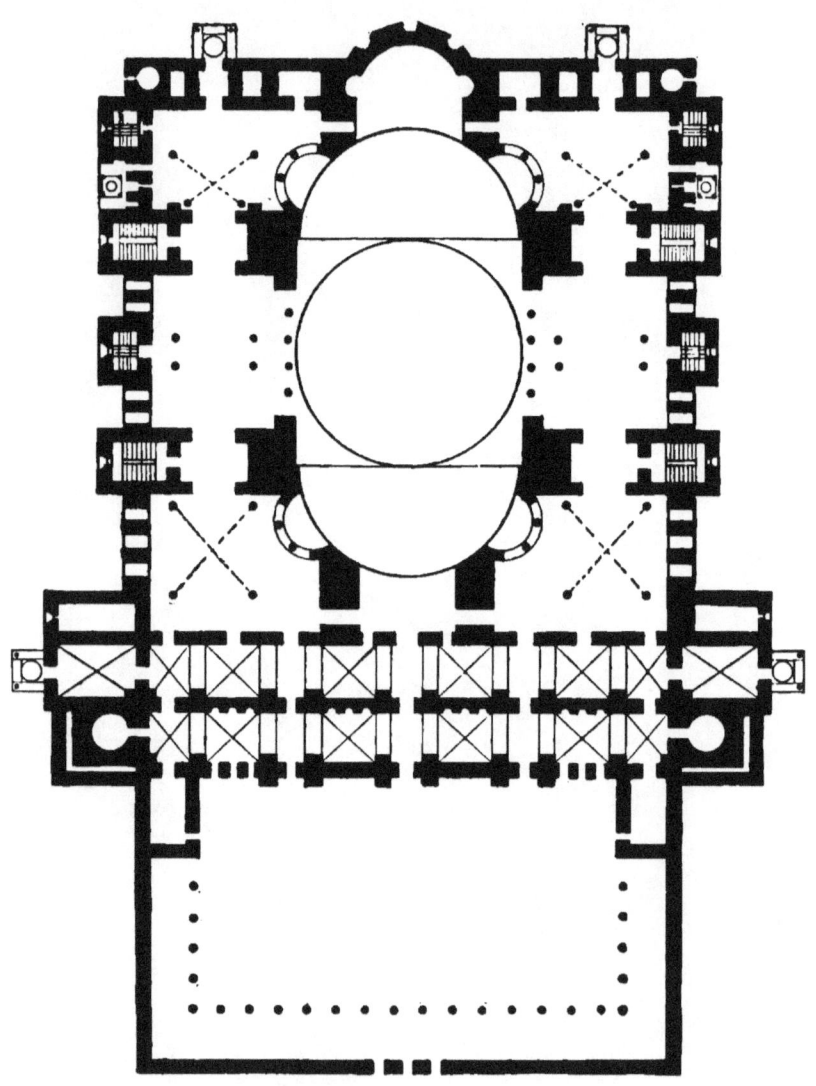

PLAN OF ST. SOPHIA, CONSTANTINOPLE.

stantine, St. Vitale, at Ravenna, and the church of Sergius and Bacchus, in the order in which they are enumerated, with that of St. Sophia, the sequence and continuous progress of domical construction is at once apparent, and such comparison explains the successive steps in a more satisfactory manner than a folio of description.

"The church of St. Sophia," says M. Texier, " is built on a square plan, 251 feet long by 186 feet wide. In the centre of this square rises the dome, the diameter of which, measuring 108 feet, determines the width of the nave. The dome is supported by four great arches and four pendentives. Two hemispheric vaults abut against the two arches, which are perpendicular to the axis of the nave, giving it an oval appearance. Each of these hemispheres is itself pierced by two smaller hemispheres carried on columns. This superposition of domes, whose points of abutment are not visible, gives to the whole structure a lightness difficult to realize."

The church is built upon a foundation of béton twenty feet deep. It is preceded by an atrium surrounded by a portico of the Ionic order. The nave is entered by a double narthex, or porch, extending along the whole width of the West front. The interior, both floor and walls, was formerly adorned with rich marbles, and paintings upon a ground of gold. The dome was built of light bricks faced with hard cement and mosaic, and was lighted by forty windows.

Originally a painting of the Holy Father was placed in the centre of the dome, and four cherubim in the pendentives. The latter are still to be discerned under the coat of whitewash with which the Turks have hidden the original magnificence of the interior.

The apse, lighted by three windows, contained the throne and seat of the Church fathers. The columns supporting the great arches and the galleries, originally occupied by the women, are of rare marble, eight of them having, it is said, formed part of the temple of Diana at Ephesus, being brought, together with the spoils of many Eastern and Western buildings, to adorn the great edifice. The foliage of their capitals is fine and sharp and intricately interlaced, having no resemblance to the Classic models beyond a debased form of the volute which terminates their upper corners. This style of ornament is a distinguishing feature of the Byzantine style, and reappears in many examples both in the East and West.

The church, commenced in the year 532, took sixteen years to build, during which time incredible sums were expended upon it. When completed, the appearance it presented was most magnificent, resulting not only from the rich marbles, wood-work, paintings, and mosaics with which it was decorated, but also from the countless candelabras, curtains, precious vases, and golden vessels with which it was furnished.

After the capture of Constantinople by Mahomet II., in the year 1453, St. Sophia was converted into a mosque, and suffered greatly at the hands of the Turks. It is only within recent years that any attempt at preserving its original splendour has been made.

The architectural principles upon which St. Sophia was constructed were reproduced in all Byzantine buildings in Italy and France as well as in the Orient. In Turkey, indeed, the edifices subsequently erected are almost counterparts of the original structure, the mosque of Suleiman and that of Achmet, built as late as 1610, embodying almost identical features of construction.

In Athens there are two or three small Byzantine churches, which, though differing greatly in point of size, are founded upon the plan of the mother church; and in Asia Minor generally and Armenia especially, there are a great number; notably the churches of Daghour and Pitzounda and the cathedral of Anim.

The decoration of some of the latter differs from the usual Byzantine methods in the frequent revival of Classic forms, and in the use of thin pilasters, carrying blind arches on the exterior.

This feature reappears in the buildings of Italy, influenced by the style, particularly at Pisa.

In some later buildings a new manner of obtaining light was introduced, by raising the dome upon a cylindrical drum, supported by the four arches and pendentives of the older system. St. Nicodemus, of Athens, is one of the best examples of this.

When the body of St. Mark was brought to Venice, having been stolen from Constantinople by means of a clever trick about the year 831, the Doge Partecipazio ordered a church to be built to his memory. The greater part of this building as it stands to-day dates, however, from the tenth century. It resembles St. Sophia in a great degree, the frequent intercourse of the Venetian maritime population with the Orient having enabled them to study the principles of Byzantine art, and to bring spoils from the buildings of the East to their native city.

St. Mark's has also much affinity with the church of Mone-tes-Koras, in Armenia, the principal façade, with its five large bays decorated with columns and arches framing the five doors which give access to the church, being identical in general conception.

The interior of the building has the form of the Greek cross, the four arms of which and also the central compartment formed by their intersection, are roofed by domes supported on arches and pendentives. The style of ornament is very similar to that of its prototype, with its rich gold mosaics, frescos, and inlaid marble, some of the details being essentially Oriental in character.

The constructors of the pendentives in St. Mark's do not seem to have properly understood that they formed part of a sphere to the centre of which their joints should have converged, but filled up the spaces between the supporting arches by a series of small superposed arches.

The influence of this Byzantine construction extended into Aquitania, in the South of France. At the close of the tenth century a number of churches were erected there, with the dome as a prominent feature. St. Front, of Perigueux, was built upon a plan closely resembling that of St. Mark's in Venice, and very nearly upon a similar scale of dimensions. The architects of the church, however, seem to have distrusted the strength of the semicircular arch, and resorted to the ogival * or pointed form as a means of securing greater supporting power, although this arch had not as yet been adopted in France.

They, too, failed completely to grasp the principle of the pendentive, as those of St. Front are formed of corbelled stones with horizontal beds, instead of voussoirs converging to the centre of the hemisphere of which they should form part.

Besides St. Front, the churches of Fontevrault, Souliac, Angoulême, and others in Aquitania were built with similar characteristics, though in plan they adopted the Latin instead of the Greek cross. The abbey church of Fontevrault is perhaps the most successful of these, the four domes of its

---

* From augere, to strengthen.

nave producing a very pleasing effect. The greater number of these buildings were erected during the eleventh and twelfth centuries, in an imported fashion, rather than in a style destined to be engrafted upon French national architecture.

All of them show the want of a clear comprehension of the principles involved, and are evidently foreign to the taste of the people.

The introduction of this style in France, offers a parallel case to the introduction of Gothic architecture in Italy, a century or two later, for in neither case were the styles in accordance with native inspiration.

VIII.

MAHOMETAN ARCHITECTURE.

THE year 622 of our era is a remarkable one in historical annals, being the date of the flight of Mahomet, the Hegira from which all events are computed by followers of his religion. Within a marvellously short period the new faith spread from the confines of Arabia, throughout Asia Minor and Persia and all along the North coast of Africa to Spain, propagated everywhere by the force of the victorious sword, until, scarcely a century later, we find its promoters bearing the crescent against Charlemagne, under the shadow of the Pyrenees.

As a political and theological narrative the history of the rise of the faith of Islam, is a wonderfully interesting one, and to us it is important as it explains the reason for the geographical position of so many buildings, erected in accordance with the requirements of the new religion, and therefore having a great similarity in all countries where it prevailed.

The Kaabah, or " square house," built by Mahomet at Mecca upon the site of a temple which tradition says was founded by Abraham, appears to have been the earliest Mahometan mosque. Mahomet had already erected a building at Medina, but this seems to have been not so much a house of prayer as a dwelling-place for his family. The Kaabah has less importance as an architectural production than as the centre of the wheel of Mahometanism, the faithful being directed to turn their faces toward it when praying, and to regard it as the ultimate goal of their wanderings.

The original structure was built by foreign workmen, and had no great pretensions, but subsequently it was surrounded by a colonnaded court, and by later additions was very considerably enlarged. Although the Koran decrees that all good Mussulmen should make a pilgrimage to Mecca, it does not uphold the Kaabah as a model to be followed in the erection of other mosques nor give any specific directions of the manner in which they should be built. It was therefore natural when the peace, following their rapid conquests, permitted the Mahometans to turn their thoughts to the erection of religious edifices, suitable for the observances of their worship, that they should borrow inspiration from the surrounding nations.

The style they eventually evolved was drawn from Byzantine, Sassanian, Greek, and Roman sources, and became native by adaptation.

In Turkey, Asia Minor, and Persia we find Mahometan mosques closely resembling Christian and Byzantine churches, many domed edifices being copied from St. Sophia and differing only in point of decoration, while the atrium or court-yard preceding the entrance to Christian buildings furnished the type for the wide colonnaded courts, with porticos roofed with a succession of hemispherical or bulbous domes, which became so common in Arabian buildings.

The mosques of Omar, at Jerusalem, on the site of the temple of Solomon, of Wallid, at Damascus, Al-Azhar, Athar-en-Neby, Ibn Touloun, and Hassan, in Cairo, are notable edifices, in which the columns are either taken or copied from Greek and Roman temples, and in which the pointed arches seem to have been suggested by the hyperbolic arches of certain ancient Sassanian structures, such as the palace of Coroes, the Takt Kesra in the ruins of Ctésiphon, on the Tigris, and the buildings of Firouzabad and Sarbistan, which were mentioned in connection with Persian art.

One of the earliest examples of the use of the pointed arch is in the Nilometer, erected on the Rodah, or Isle of Gardens, at Cairo, by Wallid, in the eighth century.

This is a matter worthy of note, as showing conclusively that the Gothic arch was no invention of the thirteenth century, in Europe, but merely the adoption of a form used five centuries before in Egypt, and probably universally known, if indeed it had ever been lost sight of, since the days of the prosperity of Babylon.

Of the early mosques the most important are those of Omar and Abd-el-Malek at Jerusalem and of Wallid at Damascus. The mosque of Omar was but a simple vaulted chamber, oriented in order to enable the faithful to turn in the direction of Mecca while praying. That of Abd-el-Malek, called the Aksah, adjoins it and is an extensive structure. It is chiefly remarkable for its general resemblance to the basilica in its division into aisles. The columns forming these carry pointed arches, built over connecting beams. It is not improbable that this design was inspired by the order of the church of the Dome of the Rock, adjoining it, built by Constantine, where the columns support circular arches, over a continuous entablature.

Wallid, Caliph of Damascus, erected a mosque on the site of the old church of St. John the Baptist, and employed labour and material in its construction furnished by Justinian, Emperor of Byzance.

The mosques of Cairo resemble each other in a great degree. They have usually a first court, giving access to apartments for the accommodation of strangers, with baths, and stables for their camels, connected with a second and larger quadrangular court, having a fountain in the centre and porticos on three sides. The fourth side, facing the entrance, has a series of aisles roofed in and forming the sanctuary, with recesses in the rear wall, where the prayers are offered. Reading-desks, provided with copies of the Koran, and hanging lamps form the chief furniture.

The minarets, one or more of which are usually

erected at the angles of the building, are special features. These tall, graceful towers, from whose summits a crier calls the people to prayers five times daily, serve a purpose similar to that of the belfries and campaniles of Europe. The diameter of most of them is small in proportion to the height, giving them a slender and beautiful aspect, very distinct from another class of towers, of which the Giralda at Seville is the best known, which were conceived in the same spirit of massiveness in which the campanile in the square before St. Mark's in Venice was built. They are ascended by spiral staircases placed either within or without, and have projecting balconies at various stages.

The building materials employed by the Arabs were chiefly stone of different colours, combined in bands and patterns, and brick covered with stucco. Enamelled tiles and multicoloured marbles were used both externally and internally, while within, carved wood, gilding, painting, and plaster were lavishly employed.

Of the forms of decoration, the chief were elaborate gold inscriptions in Arabic characters, floral and geometric designs in interlaced patterns of the most intricate combinations, coloured with all the profusion suggested by the Oriental love of brilliancy and with the exquisite harmony which we see in Persian and Indian fabrics.

A favourite form of decoration was that formed by a multiplication of minute pendentives, called the honeycomb ornament, the whole surface, as well as the dome above, being covered with an agglomeration of minute niches, the effect of which is frequently compared to that of stalactites. This form of ornament was much used, particularly in the mosques and palaces of Spain.

In Cairo domestic architecture has a distinctive character of its own. The houses have reception-rooms on the ground floor, furnished with the divans, carpets, and lamps usual in Oriental manner of life, while the upper floors, occupied by the women, have projecting balconies of lattice wood-work, which permit them to see without being seen, and form an agreeable and picturesque feature on the exterior.

The richness and the progress of Arabic art at a period when architecture had sunk to the lowest ebb throughout Europe, is due in great measure to the establishment of the learned academies of Damascus, Bagdad, and other principal cities, and to the revival of Classic learning by the translation of the works of Greek authors.

In Spain, where the Moorish and Christian populations were thrown in constant contact with one another, the difference of religious opinion maintained a wide gulf between them, and while the Christians struggled with the difficulties of the Romanesque revival, their opponents attained a brilliant era in art, as a result of their superior industry and civilization.

One of the oldest Arabian buildings in Spain is

the great mosque at Cordova. Here, as in the East, we find Corinthian and Composite columns, taken from Roman buildings on the soil, forming integral parts of the new structure, but the Classical principles of building are in no sense adhered to. The entablature is replaced by cinque-foiled arches with voussoirs of alternate stone and brick; a second order of columns is superposed directly upon the capitals of the first, carrying horseshoe arches, and between the two arcades an intermediary series of trefoiled arches is placed, springing from the keystone of the lower arches and divided at the centre by the upper ones.

The general plan of the building consists of the usual series of aisles, of which there are nineteen, with divisional walls. The sanctuary has a vault with intersecting ribs, surmounted by a small dome and enriched by profuse ornament, and is the object of much just admiration for its beauty.

The chapel of Villa Viciosa, a later structure, has a series of arcades similar to those before the sanctuary, differing only in the arrangement of the intermediary arches, which are carried up to the level of the upper arches from a horizontal course, and are cinque-foiled instead of trefoiled, both on the extrados and intrados.

The mosque was begun by Adb-el-Rhaman, in the eighth century, and successively added to during the four centuries following. It covers a very large superficial area, upwards of one hundred and sixty thousand square feet, and surpasses, in this respect, most European buildings. Its chief defects are the want of height, which does not exceed thirty feet, and the monotony of the aisles, which are nearly all precisely alike.

At Toledo there are several Moorish buildings of merit, the principal one of which is the mosque called, at present, the church of "Cristo de la Luz." It is similar to the sanctuary of Cordova in general aspect, but is a marvel of intricate and minute workmanship. The whole area which it occupies does not exceed four hundred superficial feet, but the proportions are so nicely balanced that it appears much larger. There are four columns carrying horseshoe arches, above which comes a second arcade, and each division is roofed in by a vault of intersecting ribs. These vaults are formed of wood, overlaid with plaster, and have no pretension to scientific construction. Indeed, in none of the Arabian buildings in Spain do we find anything of the kind attempted, the decorative features being always the most prominent.

In the tower of Seville a species of vault was formed by thickening the walls gradually as they rose from the ground until they met; this, however, was nothing more than extensive corbelling, and, consequently, very inferior to Roman and Byzantine methods.

The Alcázar, at Seville, and the Palace of the Alhambra, at Granada, are the richest examples of

Moorish architecture, and show in their design and ornament the most fertile expression of the brilliant imagination with which this warm-blooded people imbued all its creations.

The Court of the Lions in the latter, a rectangular enclosure, surrounded by arcades, with projecting domed pavilions at the upper and lower ends, is generally held to be the finest production of the later period of the style.

The same materials are used here as in the other buildings—plaster shaped in the most exquisite forms and coloured brilliantly, tiles ornamented with patterns and devices of the most elaborate character, and wooden ceilings carved and richly painted. All these are handled with such correct taste that their brilliancy never degenerates into gaudiness.

A splendid fountain in the centre of the court, the lower bowl of which is supported upon the backs of lions, explains the name given to this celebrated structure.

The mosque of Cordova is superior, in respect to materials, to the other remaining Moorish buildings in Spain, in which plaster is used to excess. It is vain, however, to look in any of them for any distinct or novel constructional departure. The lintel and arch in Greece and Rome, the dome carried on pendentives in Byzance, were features giving character to each style, but the art of the Mahometan architects differed only in form and colour from its predecessors. The horseshoe arch with one and two centres, that is both round and pointed, was used by them almost exclusively, but it cannot rank as a constructional invention, for the real arch starts only at the level of the centres, and the remaining lower portion is a mere corbelling to obtain a form pleasing to the eye.

Any new method of construction always affected the surrounding parts, and often altered the whole design of a building. It is obvious, therefore, that a mere change in the appearance of an arch such as this, which affects nothing connected with it, cannot be said to have created any new era in the progress of building.

We hear the question frequently asked why a modern and new style is not developed in our times, and the answer architects make is illustrated by just this case, that is, that no new style can be evolved without a new constructive principle. As yet none such has been forthcoming, the only novel method of construction lately introduced being the employment of iron girders and posts, which, from an artistic point of view, can scarcely be considered an improvement upon the use of what are called the natural building materials.

IX.

THE ROMANESQUE STYLE.

SOME late historians have departed from the previously generally accepted nomenclature of architectural styles, in designating under the general term of Christian architecture all buildings erected between the tenth and sixteenth centuries in Western Europe.

As, however, Christian building in Europe began with the conversion of Constantine, this chronology is hardly satisfactory, and as the customary division of Gothic from the styles preceding it, is on many grounds a convenient one, it is preferable to adopt the conventional names, and to distinguish under the title of "Romanesque" the outgrowth of the debased form of Roman architecture which, influenced by Byzantine and Arabic art, formed a distinct method of building throughout the West for nearly two centuries after the year 1000 A.D., giving it the alternative name of "Norman" in Normandy and England.

Previous to this date the long continuance of war and barbaric incursions seem to have prevented the erection of any stable edifices; fire and the poverty of the material with which they were constructed having caused the destruction of the few of which an account has been preserved.

Many churches subsequently built, however, were erected upon the sites of these older ones and have fragments of the older buildings incorporated in them. Of such are the churches of St. Germain des Prés, in Paris, and Notre Dame du Port, at Clermont.

Under Charlemagne, a revival of art was attempted, the chief building constructed by him being a reproduction of St. Vitale, of Ravenna, in which he employed sculpture and ornament torn from the original structure, and fragments from the edifices of ancient Rome; but this effort soon died away, and the period intervening between the eighth and tenth centuries was totally lacking in any architectural production of merit.

As the Roman principles of architecture had been taken Eastward and gradually transformed into a new style at Byzance, so also in the West they had been the forerunners of another method of building, but proportionately different in accordance with the character, customs, and race of the Western populations.

The basilica formed, as it had in the East, the model upon which all church architecture was designed, the nave, transept, aisles, and apse being all retained in this new class of buildings, but many of the building methods were new, and the details of their decoration differed considerably from the precise proportions and Classic graces of the buildings of Rome. The result exhibits a curious contrast between the barbaric ornament and the scientific construction, which advanced throughout the style in the genuine efforts which were made to progress in the art of building.

Starting thus at the decadence of Classic art, with a Classical building as the original type for their churches, the Romanesque architects took up each of the parts combining in its formation, and sought to improve or elaborate each, in pursuance of certain ends, arising from local necessities. There is virtually no point where Romanesque ends and Gothic commences, to give due reason for the conventional divisions of historians, for the one style melts into the other in the continual progress in the study of the principles of construction which was steadily effected throughout both styles.

They differ chiefly in that, during the two centuries prior to the thirteenth century, the pointed arch was rarely used, and that the influence of the Classic decadence is more apparent in the buildings of the earlier period. After this, the pointed arch became universal, and the whole style becoming entirely distinct from its derivation, the ornament and detail, quite unlike anything which had come before, it may be said that a new style had been created.

This new style, which has been called Gothic,

continued to be developed until the fifteenth century, when its principles became exaggerated, and it died out at the extreme point to which they could be pushed.

It has been customary to call the buildings of the eleventh and twelfth centuries, built in the transition of Roman to Gothic art, Romanesque; but the pointed arch was used in both styles, though, as stated above, less frequently in the earlier one; and it should not, therefore, be taken as the distinguishing characteristic of Gothic architecture.

The chief points wherein the Romanesque churches, which were the only buildings of importance constructed at that period, differed from the basilicas were in the methods of vaulting and their consequent effects upon the whole structure, the elaboration of the apse, and the system of connected supports employed. The main characteristics of the style were the same in all Western countries, and these being known, it is not difficult to distinguish the slight differences arising from local causes.

In the old basilicas the aisles, whether of one or two stories, were lighted by windows in the lateral walls, while the nave borrowed light from them, and also received it directly from a clere-story rising above the roof of the galleries. As we have seen, these buildings were usually covered by wooden roofs, tunnel-vaults or a series of intersecting vaults thrown across the square formed by two of the columns of the nave, equidistant from each other and from corresponding pilasters in the side walls, being only occasionally used in the aisles.

The Western architects of the tenth century continued to build their churches in this manner, and we have a splendid example of a timber roof of this kind, as late even as the twelfth century, in Peterborough Cathedral; but at an early period they sought to replace these perishable roofs by stone vaults. They found the construction of the semi-dome of the apse and the vaulting of the side aisles, either by a continuous tunnel-vault, by a series of semicircular vaults perpendicular to the lateral walls, or by intersecting vaults upon a square plan, comparatively easy; but the vaulting of the nave was a much more difficult matter.

The circular tunnel-vault would have been the simplest known method of accomplishing this, but the pressure of a circular vault placed over the nave would have tended to push outward the walls upon which it rested, and this pressure being continuous, it was obviously of no avail to place buttresses at any separate point, and to place a great number, side by side, all along the vault, or, in other words, to greatly thicken the supporting wall, was to take up too much valuable ground space.

In St. Front and kindred structures we have seen the problem solved in one way by the introduction of Byzantine domes; but these churches were confined to a province of Southern France, and had but little influence in other districts.

In St. Etienne de Nevers, St. Sernin de Toulouse, and in Notre Dame du Port at Clermont in Auvergne, and others, this difficulty is partially overcome by the building of a half vault over the upper galleries connecting the tunnel-vault of the nave with the outer main walls, and taking the strain continuously, the thickness of the outer wall not being considered of consequence. This system permitted the placing of roofing-tiles directly upon the extrados of the vaults, and the entire suppression of wooden rafters, which was advantageous in diminishing the risk of fire, although the pitch was scarcely sufficient to prevent leakage. The great disadvantage, however, was that the nave had only borrowed light, and in large churches it was inconveniently dark.

Another method adopted was that of suppressing the upper gallery, and bringing the arches of the aisles up to the level of the springing of the main vault, so that the summits of the side vaults and the walls erected between them, which were at right angles to the nave, served to counteract the strain of the upper vault. We have examples of this in the cathedral of Limoges and at Fontenay, but it is open to the same objection, that of darkening the nave.

Still another system consisted in binding the vault over the nave by ribs or arches thrown across to opposite piers, which were strengthened by buttresses. These buttresses, however, were

ELEVATION.

ROMANESQU

SECTION.

built upon the top of the arches, thrown across the aisles, and did more harm than good.

There is an example of unusual construction at Tournus, in Burgundy, where the difficulty is effectually surmounted by the building of a number of arches at right angles to the axis of the nave, between each set of piers; but the effect is far from satisfactory.

Finally at Vezelay, in France, the tunnel-vault was abandoned and diagonal intersecting vaults were thrown across the nave, framed in between semicircular arch ribs carried upon piers spaced at equal intervals, the weight being thus wholly transferred to the four points at the angles of each compartment. It was found, however, that these piers needed strengthening, as the strain upon them was excessive, and it was thus that external buttresses were resorted to, which were connected with the piers by arches, called flying buttresses, bridging the side aisles and conveying the pressure to the outer wall. A weight was placed over each buttress, generally taking the form of a pinnacle, which stiffened it and counteracted the pressure of the arch.

An illustration of this mode of construction has been attempted in the accompanying drawing, which does not represent any special building, but in which the chief characteristics of the style at this juncture have been introduced.

The distance across the nave being usually greater than that between the columns dividing it from the aisles, the rectangular compartments of the vault were consequently no longer square, but oblong, so that while the arches crossing the nave at right angles were still semicircular those between the pillars were pointed.

The transition from this, in the thirteenth century, to the definite adoption of the pointed vault was consequently but a step.

We see, thus, that a continual progress was made in vaulting throughout the style, and the principle of concentrating weight upon isolated points was evolved in order to vault the nave and at the same time give direct light to it. In effecting this result, however, the original aim had been lost sight of—namely, that of avoiding the use of wooden roofs; for when the Romanesque architects abandoned tunnel-vaulting they had to surmount their more complicated intersecting vaults by wooden roofs, the perishable nature of which caused the ruin of many of the finest buildings. Nor was the external appearance of these roofs any improvement upon those of St. Etienne and St. Sernin, for it is a question whether any more monumental roof has been conceived than that which is formed by the natural outside surface of stone vaults.

In the old basilicas, columns taken from or modelled upon those of the temples and palaces of Rome had sufficed to support the light brick wall, carried upon an architrave or arches, which enclosed the nave. When the Western architects resumed the building of churches, after an interval of war and trouble which had proved fatal to architectural progress, brick was little used and the formation of light masonry and good mortar were lost arts. The slender Classic column was consequently insufficient to carry the load of a heavy stone wall and had, necessarily, to be replaced by a more solid pier.

These piers assumed various forms in the tentative efforts made to construct them of the dimensions calculated to occupy the least amount of floor space; some were square, others circular or formed of a number of small columns grouped together, but for a long time no very satisfactory shape was found which avoided a clumsy adjustment of the superstructure.

It came to be gradually recognized that the form of the pier should be subservient to, and made to correspond with, the arches and the column receiving the arch rib of the vault above, which it had to sustain. This was effected at first by a square pier, with rectangular projections on each side, forming abutments for the reception of the constructional arrangement above. Subsequently these were replaced by pilasters and engaged columns on each face, three of which supported the rear and side arches of the nave, the fourth being continued up to the springing of the vault, and redeemed from exaggerated effect by bands or string-courses. There are good examples in France at Vezelay, Beaune and Langres and Autun. In England the contemporary architects usually employed square or circular masses of solid masonry, carrying a heavy abacus, these pillars being sometimes ornamented with a fluting, as in the crypt at Canterbury, or with zigzag patterns, as at Waltham Abbey, Durham, and Lindisfarne.

The capitals of Romanesque columns are especially interesting, for they became constructively useful instead of simply ornamental, as were those used in the Roman orders. The section of the arch rib being square and the column round, it was necessary to afford support to the overlapping corners, the whole surface of the projecting tile or abacus being occupied by the upper masonry, instead of the line of the shaft being continued up, as had been done in Rome. The capital was therefore made to spread outward from the shaft in order to corbel the superstructure.

A simple form of this is found in many German, Italian, and English examples, the upper part of the capital being a cube and the lower a hemisphere. The early examples generally imitate those of the Corinthian order in a rude fashion corresponding with the poverty of talent of the period. The capitals of the twelfth century are better carved and better suited to the services they have to perform. Figures representing biblical subjects are introduced in some and in others strange animals and conventional foliage, sometimes arranged as the acanthus leaf had been in the Roman models. The proportions

1. Greek Lintel.   2. Roman Arch, showing

4. Arch Springing from Column.   5. Romanesque Column, with Arches Springing from Outer Edge of the Capital.

COMPARATIVE SERIES, SHOWING GREEK, RO

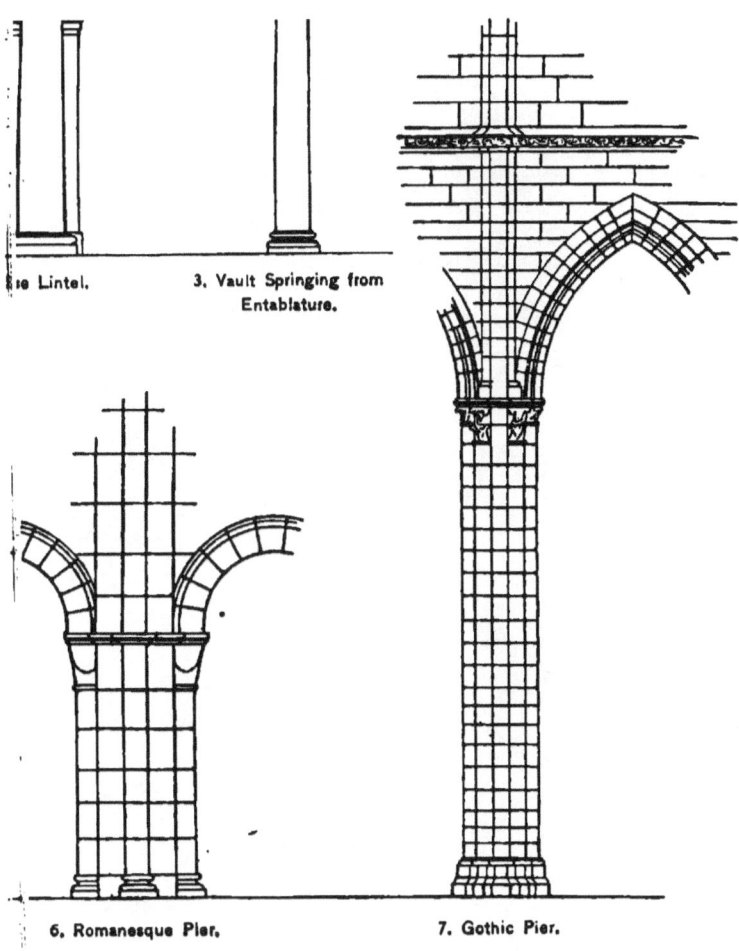

ie Lintel.   3. Vault Springing from Entablature.

6. Romanesque Pier.   7. Gothic Pier.

ROMANESQUE, AND GOTHIC METHODS OF SUPPORT.

of the Classic column were also departed from, the capital often being a quarter or a sixth of the whole column; its height being regulated by the size of the beds of stone, which were generally low. In Germany, however, the older proportions were more closely adhered to. The quality of the stone determined in a great measure the depth of the carving, the harder kinds having less depth of incision and the style of ornament applied to them resembling the Byzantine.

In France the Romanesque column has usually a third of the diameter of its shaft engaged in a pier or wall, though isolated ones are used in the triforiums, towers, and porches; in England the latter are common, and recessed columns, that is to say, placed in an angle of masonry, are also frequently seen.

The bases of Romanesque columns, at first simple round and hollow moulds, gradually became more elaborate, until they resembled the attic base. Occasionally they were decorated with foliage or animals, and there are instances where both capital and base are similar. The introduction of an angle ornament, connecting the torus or round mould with the corners of the plinth beneath, is especially noticeable; this was effective in preventing the angles from being broken by thickening the stone at the weakest points, and in later examples added to the beauty of the base.

The arches of the period were usually semicircular

and employed either separately or with a second and broader one, their contour being frequently marked by a few simple mouldings of degenerate classic origin.

Two or three arches supported by detached columns, and comprised within a larger one, were frequently placed in the triforiums; when three were used the central one was usually higher than the others. Besides mouldings: billets, zigzags, stars, and similar simple ornaments weer employed in their decoration. Where Arabic taste exercised its influence, it is not uncommon to find alternate voussoirs of different-coloured stones, and variegated bands in the piers.

The Italians were especially fond of this treatment and it is seen in the exteriors and interiors of many of their buildings. To them is also due the introduction of blind arcades, the columns of which were either engaged in the wall or separated from it by an intervening gallery. The façade of the cathedral at Pisa is perhaps the most beautiful example of this.

In the West, arcades of this kind became a frequent method of decorating blank walls, and there are instances where a second series of arches intersect the first, resulting in a number of pointed arches formed by the crossing of the circular ones; from this an ingenious but unfounded theory has been deducted purporting to explain the origin of Gothic architecture.

The doors and porches of the Romanesque period

are among the most beautiful to be found in any style. Starting in the earlier examples with a simple, round-arched opening, the number of mouldings in the arch became richer and of greater number, and, as the style advanced, recessed and supported by columns. These mouldings were decorated with the zigzag, billet, and kindred ornaments, many of which were probably copied from the decoration of the old basilica of St. Paul's without the walls of Rome.

As the jambs of the doorways were generally built on an angle, the contiguous shafts and arches sometimes gave the effect of an arched passage in perspective. Such effects were frequently intentional in the churches in Southern France, for we find that the walls of the nave and vault of Notre Dame de Poitiers, and of other buildings, were purposely made to converge in order to give the appearance of greater length.

It was not uncommon to give the doors square heads, supported by corbels and occasionally by a central shaft; in these cases the arch above relieved the lintel from the weight of the superstructure, and gave the character of the style to the whole. The tympanum, thus enclosed, offered a ground for rich sculpture, which was availed of to the fullest extent. The outer door of a porch was usually richer in design than the inner one; in England there are many examples of shallow porches with single deeply recessed doors.

In Provence there are many beautiful examples, foremost amongst which must be mentioned the porch of St. Trophyme, at Arles (see frontispiece). Romanesque windows were but modifications of the doors; often having recessed shafts at their sides and being frequently divided by a central column.

The bull's-eye, or round window, of the early Christian basilicas continued to be used, but it had not as yet the richness of tracery which it attained in the Gothic period.

Classical features of design still retained their hold upon many details, notably in the cornices, where the modillions or brackets of the Corinthian order were frequently employed, and but slightly altered in form, although of native composition. The corona of the cornice also differed but little from the Roman models, and was occasionally supported directly by engaged columns replacing buttresses, chiefly on the exterior of apsidal chapels.

In the early Christian churches the apse had consisted of a central semicircular termination to the building, flanked occasionally by two smaller semicircular recesses containing altars. In the baptisteries and Byzantine churches these had been multiplied, and had come to be customary features in every new building. In England, the Norman architects generally ended their churches rectangularly, without even the original single apse, though there are a few examples in which it is used, as at Newhaven, Sussex. In Germany it was frequent-

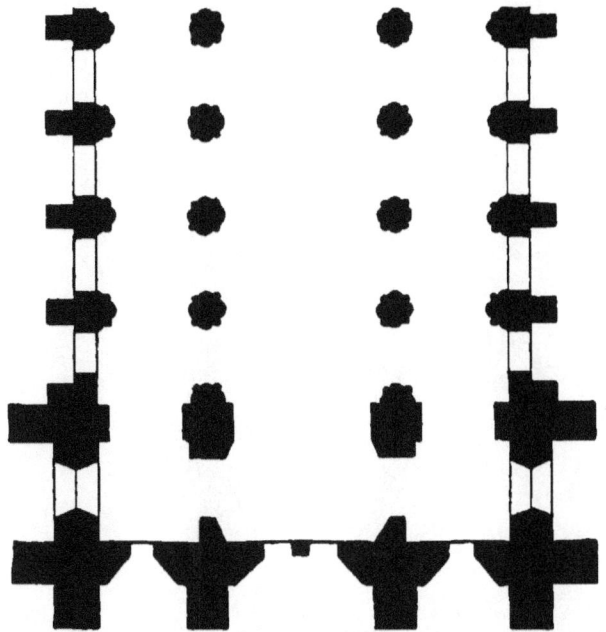

PLAN OF STRASBOURG CATHEDRAL. (Compare with Basilica, page 89.)

ly the custom to affix apses to three sides of the square tower placed at the intersection of the nave and transept, and the result was generally satisfactory, as may be seen in St. Martin's of Cologne, and in the Apostles' Church in the same city.

In France the plan resolved itself into an open semicircular colonnade with a passage intervening between it and the outer wall which followed the outline of a series of small apses. These formed an harmonious cluster, and became a type which was matured in the thirteenth and fourteenth centuries. Those belonging to the Romanesque period, however, had a distinct and constructively excellent character which has rarely been subsequently surpassed. Among the best are those of Notre Dame du Port at Clermont, St. Etienne de Nevers, and St. Sernin at Toulouse.

In France towers were generally placed at the West end of the church, while in England and Germany the usual way was to build them at the junction of the nave and transept; in Italy they were often detached from the main structure. They were characterized by simple solidity; the openings being few and the detail bold; the angles were strengthened by stout piers; the roofs were either of timber or stone, according to the nature of the materials in the localities in which they were erected, and they were usually lighted by the round-arched double window. This round arch, ornamented with a few simple mouldings and reposing upon short sturdy columns, forms a constantly recurring feature in the composition of the several parts of Romanesque buildings.

The corridors which surrounded the square courtyards adjoining churches, and connected them with the dormitories, refectories, and other apartments of the clergy, are called cloisters. They differed but little from the Roman "impluvium" and the "atrium" of the basilica, the changes consisting chiefly in the addition of raised sills separating them from the court, and in their being usually vaulted instead of carrying timber roofs. The series of arcades forming them were treated in many ways, and the detail admitted of much elaboration and variety, as may be seen in the many remarkable examples throughout Europe. The cloisters of St. Paul's, at Rome, and the atrium of St. Ambrogio, at Milan, form very interesting historical links between the Roman and Romanesque styles and are very beautiful specimens of their kind.

It had been the custom during the struggling period of the early Church to bury the bodies of saints in subterranean chambers called crypts, a word derived from the Greek verb "to hide"; subsequently these became component parts of all churches, serving as places of interment and for the occasional celebration of masses. Their masonry was necessarily of the massive character required for the foundation of the piers of the church above,

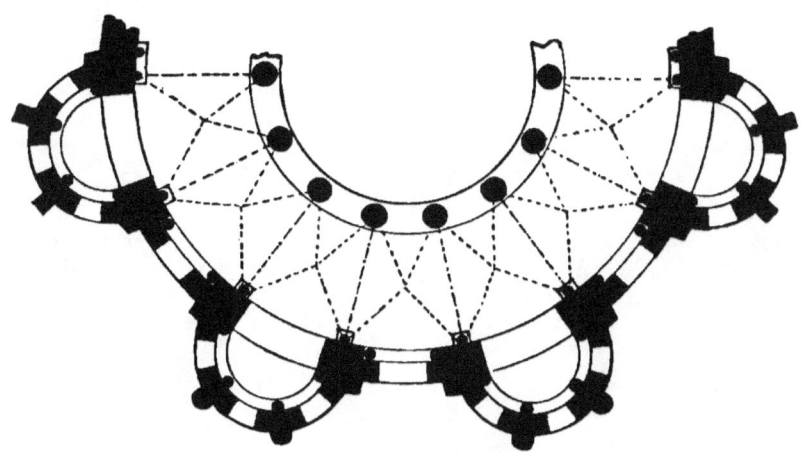

CHEVET OF NOTRE DAME DU PORT AT CLERMONT.

(*From Chapuy.*)

consisting generally in a grouping of columns sustaining a heavy vault.

The crypt of St. Eutrope, at Saintes in France, may be mentioned as one of the best examples, the pillars being richly carved, and the ribs of the vault of great boldness and strength.

In Germany the crypt is often raised sufficiently above the level of the ground to obtain light from windows, as at Spires, and this is sometimes carried to such an extreme that the church becomes double, that is, of two stories, as at Schwartz Rheindorf.

In England, Canterbury Cathedral possesses perhaps the best example, the crypt being very large and its details varied. Some of the capitals of the columns remain half finished, the work upon them having been arrested by a conflagration in the twelfth century.

X.

GOTHIC ARCHITECTURE.

BRIEFLY recapitulating the preceding chapters: We have seen that the Greek temple, composed of a cella, or oblong room, surrounded by a colonnade, was copied by the Romans with but few alterations, the only one of importance being the addition of a semicircular recess to the rear wall. The columns of the colonnade having been transposed from the outside to the interior, dividing the room in three parts, longitudinally; a cross wall having been introduced dividing it transversely, and the apse retained, the building became a basilica. By extending the transept and nave the plan became cruciform and symbolically the most suitable for that of a Christian church.

The Western architects, desiring to replace the wooden roofs by stone vaults, found it convenient to substitute for columns carrying arches, piers with engaged shafts connecting directly with the superstructure.

After various attempts to obtain direct light for the central division or nave, rendered difficult by the necessity of counteracting the continuous thrust of the barrel vault thrown across it, this vault was finally abandoned and replaced by intersecting vaults, which conveyed the thrust diagonally upon equidistant piers. To avoid increasing the size of the latter to an inconvenient extent, an expedient was resorted to which consisted in propping them from the exterior by flying buttresses thrown from them to outside piers across the roof of the aisles. The result of the width of the nave being usually greater than the distance between piers was that, while the diagonal ribs of the vault remained semicircular, their lateral intersection produced pointed arches.

This form of construction was developed during the middle and latter half of the twelfth century. The pointed arch had been used occasionally before by the Romanesque architects; it had been used frequently by the Arabs, as far back as the eighth century, and had been known and employed long before the Christian era in the sewers of Babylon. It was, therefore, not a new invention, but a known method adopted in a fresh departure in constructive architecture; for the circular arches being abandoned and definitely replaced by the pointed arch the succeeding architecture became pointed or Gothic.

This is the condensed history of the derivation of the style as generally accepted at the present day, though the subject has given rise to much controversy.

The concentration of the weight of the vault upon the piers, instead of upon a continuous wall, was more or less the key to the whole scheme of Gothic construction; for the main principle remained the same throughout its many and varied examples. The idea was improved upon gradually and finally pushed to exaggeration; the decoration of the component parts of a building increased as the style advanced and they were reduced to just the sizes needed for stability, but their construction remained almost unaltered throughout.

We have followed the steps by which the form given to Christian churches emanated from the early basilicas; this form of building, that is, its plan and divisions into nave, aisles, transept, choir, apse, etc., had become traditional and was generally accepted in all the best examples.

The problem of accommodating large assemblies in the manner best suited to enable them to concentrate their sight and hearing upon a given point has been solved in various ways, perhaps most successfully in our modern opera-houses, but this problem was not one with which the Gothic architects endeavoured to grapple; their attention was devoted to the improvement and embellishment of the typical plan of structure, which custom and dogma had prescribed as the most suitable and in accordance with the needs of the liturgy. The plan was more or less elastic, and differed without material distinction in the different countries of Western Europe. These differences are easily noted by comparing the appended plans; the one, that of Rheims Cathe-

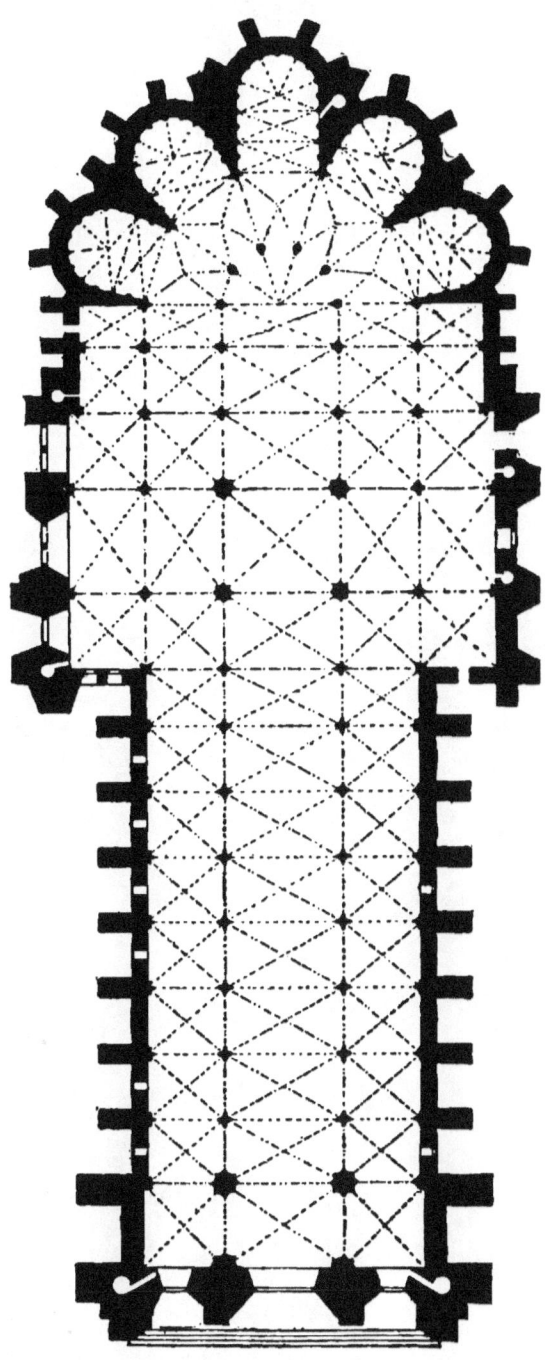

PLAN OF RHEIMS CATHEDRAL.

dral, showing perhaps the most perfect arrangement of any in France, and the other, that of a typical English cathedral. The latter does not represent any particular structure, but is a composition including all the usual divisions and connecting buildings, taken from an old copy of Rickman.

 $a, a,$ Towers at West end.
 $b, b,$ Porches.
  $c,$ The nave.
 $d, d,$ Side aisles of the nave.
  $e,$ The cloisters.
  $f,$ Library.
  $g,$ North transept.
  $h,$ South transept.
  $i, i,$ Side aisles of South transept.
$k, k, k,$ Chapels.
  $l,$ Chapter house with passage from the cloisters.
  $m,$ Central tower, cross or lantern.
  $n,$ Screen, over which the organ is usually placed.
  $o,$ Choir, at the east end of which the altar is usually placed.
 $p, p,$ Side aisles of the choir.
  $q,$ Lady chapel.

In the thirteenth century the style was formed in all its purity; it was characterized by great simplicity and beauty, and in these respects was never surpassed. The arch had few mouldings, and these clearly defined and graceful; the shafts of columns were of slender and charming proportions, and the foliage employed for the decoration of their capitals, while conventional, departed entirely from the acanthus leaves of Classic origin, and assumed forms suggested by Western plants.

Piers were reduced to the precise dimensions needful, and were formed of slender shafts, grouped together, which received the arch mouldings on either side, and rose in the front and rear to the height necessary to take the springing of the vault. In practice, the thrust of the vault was found not to be transmitted directly to a point to be received by an arch, but to two points above and below this theoretical one, which necessitated the employment of two flying buttresses, the one above the other. In Chartres Cathedral these are connected by radiating columns, and there are many examples where the intervening space is occupied by an open arcade. The French generally built their vertical buttresses very massively, but in England the pinnacle was more frequently used to counteract the thrust of the arch. For this purpose it was eminently appropriate, and might be considered ornamental, but the placing of pinnacles upon the corners of the towers and elsewhere where they served no end, which was often done, was always a mistake; and a defect which mars the effect of many beautiful English buildings.

In Notre Dame of Paris, we find the single round column still occupying the first story, with the more complex arrangement of pier and connected shafts starting above the abacus of its capital, but as a general thing, a distinct shaft was provided for each set of mouldings. In time this was replaced by a continuation of the vault mouldings down to

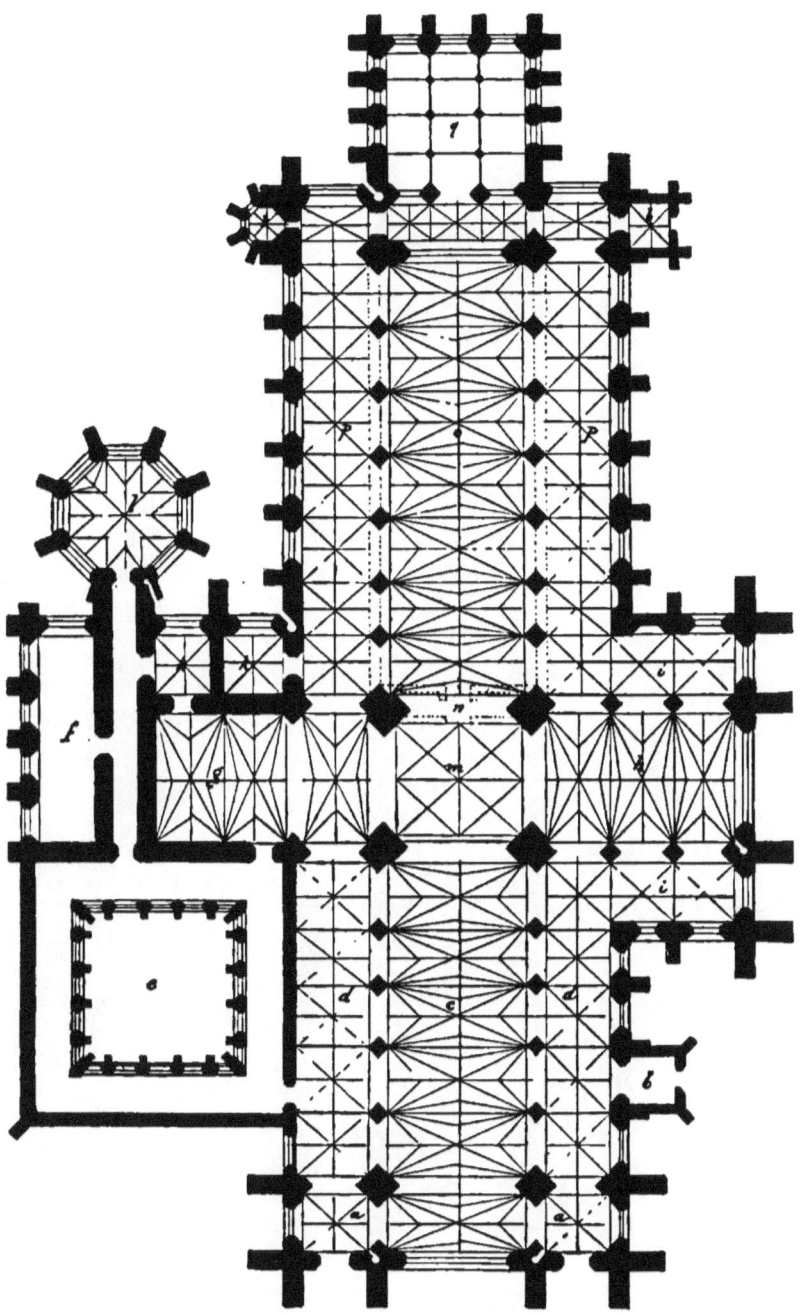

PLAN OF AN ENGLISH CATHEDRAL.

(*From Rickman.*)

the floor, interrupted only by an occasional string-course, or a band of foliage replacing the capital.

Once the weight of the vault had been transferred to piers, the wall connecting them ceased to support anything but the extremity of the cross-vault comprised between the piers, and otherwise served only as a screen. The Gothic architects soon took advantage of this to widen the windows, which had been narrow in the early stages, for by throwing a discharging arch just under the upper vault across the piers the whole space underneath could be occupied by windows, which, with the improvement in the making of painted glass, became extremely desirable. This was accordingly done, the only stonework left being the network of mullions and tracery necessary to receive the panes. This tracery, probably suggested by the rich Arabic window fillings, made a great advance during the latter part of the thirteenth and fourteenth centuries, the combinations of geometrical figures, chiefly the circle, being often wonderfully beautiful. The rose window was much favoured by the French in their West fronts and transepts, but in England the large pointed window was generally preferred, and admirably suited the square termination of the apse, which was the most frequently used in that country.

The space enclosed by the pointed window had an outline to which it was always difficult to adjust geometric traceries so as to avoid clumsy joints, or oddly shaped patterns, and these were, therefore, subsequently replaced by flowing lines, which could be used with much greater freedom.

As these grew bolder they assumed a flame-like appearance, and the later period of the style to which they belong was, in consequence, called "Flamboyant." This development occurred chiefly in France, some of the best examples being in the church of St. Ouen, at Rouen.

The simplest form of the Gothic vault was that in which the compartment comprised between two piers on one side and two on the opposite side of the nave was marked by two ribs bridging it, and two diagonal ribs intersecting each other. As the system advanced the vault became more complex by the addition of other ribs, as strengtheners or as ornaments, until in some examples the whole vault became a network of intersecting ribs.

These intersections were frequently emphasized by a keystone or by an ornament called a boss, which in English work was also placed at intervals along string-courses, breaking the continuity after the manner of modillions in Classic cornices.

A keystone placed in the centre of a vault was held there by a combination of great strength, as it became a point of abutment for all the main ribs, whose thrust was distributed against four piers and hence exteriorly by buttresses to the ground. A good stone, therefore, in this position could have extraordinary dimensions, and was susceptible of a variety of treatment. In some French examples it was extended, or rather hung, considerably below the surface of the vault and ornamentally carved, while in England, in the late so-called Perpendicular Gothic, it formed the centre of a large pendant, or circular hanging ornament, which in some cases came down almost to the level of the springing of the ribs.

This construction was used chiefly in connection with the fan-vaulting, in which English architects excelled, which may indeed be said to be an English invention and monopoly, as no examples of it are found elsewhere. The name explains, in measure, the form taken by the ribs, which, spreading out from the sheaf of mouldings in the pier, trace a perfect semicircle on the upper ceiling, their intervening spaces being occupied by panels. The four semicircles thus traced by the ribs, starting from four piers of a compartment, are each tangent to a central and whole circle forming the contour of the pendant.

To be successful this requires that the compartment or space included between four piers, two on each side of the nave or choir, should be a square, otherwise the circles do not touch, and the lines are inharmonious.

The chapels of Henry the Seventh, at Westminster, and of St. George, at Windsor, contain the best examples of fan-vaulting, and are very beautiful in general effect, though it is questionable whether such constructive tricks are worthy of unrestricted praise, while the abuse of panelling in which English architects indulged in these later Gothic buildings, by which the whole wall and ceiling surface was cut up in an unending repetition, was certainly blameworthy, and tended to reduce their art to a mechanical science.

They excelled, however, in all mechanical workmanship, in which perhaps that employed in the execution of timber roofs is the most remarkable. These were in a measure, at least upon so large a scale, a feature wholly English, for nothing approaching them is found elsewhere. The roof of Westminster Hall is the most justly celebrated and is unique in general character.

The natural stonework showing all its joints was generally left untouched in the interior of Gothic buildings, and afforded the best finish as well as contrast to the stained glass in the windows.

Polychrome decoration was attempted occasionally, chiefly on the Continent, and in some instances successfully. The best examples are the restorations of the Ste. Chapelle and St. Germain des Prés, in Paris, though the latter belongs more properly to the Romanesque period. Many churches have been completely spoiled as regards their inside appearance by coats of whitewash applied to the whole interior surface, giving them a bleak and barn-like aspect fatal to architectural effect; this is especially frequent in Belgium.

This whitewash, coupled with horribly incongruous late Renaissance decoration, has gone far in many cases to ruin what would otherwise be fine buildings.

Externally all *good* Gothic buildings showed a direct correspondence with the interior: buttresses, flying buttresses, pinnacles, etc., were all constructive and never decorative devices; there was never such a thing as a façade or false front built independently of the interior, and though the harmony of the lines of both were often difficult to reconcile, it was just in the overcoming of such difficulties that the brilliant qualities of Gothic architects were called forth.

In the arrangement of the West fronts the French were at their best, for the combination of deeply recessed porches with the rose window and gable above, flanked by the towers, which in France were usually placed here, was both judicious and effective. In England such porches as those of Rheims, or deep openings, such as the entrances to the cathedral of Paris, were not used, and the West elevations are consequently less interesting. Peterborough is an exception to this rule, but the design is so exaggerated, that the three immense arcades dwarf everything connected with them.

The custom of placing a tower and spire over the intersection of the nave and transept was always adhered to in England, and was always a happy arrangement which gave the building dignity and character, even when the Western towers were omitted. Of this the celebrated Salisbury Cathedral is a beautiful example.

The spires of Chartres and of St. Ouen, at Rouen, are the finest in France, where towers were frequently built to receive spires which were never added. The height to which the nave was carried there often prevented the towers from having their due effect, as it was impossible to carry them out on a scale large enough to give them a corresponding proportion. English architects contented themselves with moderate interior heights, rendering the proportioning of their buildings a much easier task than that which their neighbours imposed upon themselves, by attempting with each new building a more daring altitude, until the crumbling vaults of Beauvais set a limit to their audacity.

The comparison of contemporary Gothic in England and France covers the subject more accurately than between that of any other countries, for these two nations rivalled each other all along in the solution of the various problems which arose with each step in their progress, while the architects of other countries profited by the results they attained and erected their buildings on Anglo-French principles.

The cathedrals of Cologne, in Germany, and Toledo, in Spain, are as fine as any to be found in France or England, but they are neither German nor Spanish in conception and principle, and therefore do not belong to the national architecture of these countries.

it has a cloister with traceried windows, which, notwithstanding its round arches, more nearly resembles Northern Gothic than anything in Italy, and by its greater height shows a novel and more effective treatment than is usually seen in France or England.

The little church of St. Maria della Spina in this town, on the banks of the Arno, is a charming little edifice of the Sienna type.

In civil architecture Italy has much to boast of. Her palaces and fortresses are amongst the noblest and most picturesque buildings of the Middle Ages found anywhere in Europe. Most of these are rectangular masses of stone, the austerity of which is relieved by heavy window-openings with pointed heads and moulded frames, and crowned by a battlemented cornice, occasionally enlivened by shields placed between alternate corbels. The addition of the campanile, used as a lookout tower rather than as a belfry, generally completes an imposing structure.

Of those in stone, the Palazzo Vecchio and the Bargello, in Florence, are among the finest of these half town-hall, half fortress buildings, while the Municipio of Sienna, with its immensely high campanile, may be mentioned as typical of those in brick. Nearly every large city possesses one of these tall towers, notably Verona, Cremona, Mantua, and Florence. In the last named the tower of Giotto is the most highly ornamented and graceful of this class of structure, and for general proportions unsurpassed. Longfellow, in his well-known poem, regrets the lack of a spire to complete it, but it is questionable whether such an addition could have been made in keeping with the style in which it is designed.

In France the lately restored Chateau de Pierrefonds, near Compiegne, illustrates, perhaps as well as any, the typical military building of the Gothic period, with all the usual accompanying structures. The exterior walls are high and massive, with round towers at the angles crowned with projecting battlements and conical roofs. An interior court is reached only by traversing a drawbridge and passing through an outer gate and passage defended by heavy portcullis. Around this court are grouped the apartments, banqueting halls, the chapel, and the necessary quarters for residents and garrison.

The number of remaining domestic buildings of the period is comparatively limited. The house of Jacques Coeur at Bourges, the monastic Hotel de Cluny, in Paris, the Palais de Justice, and the Hotel Bourgtheroulde, in Rouen, may be mentioned among the few still standing, as the best examples of contemporary architecture.

Of small half-timbered houses there remain a fair number in France, though they are daily being demolished, in the principal cities, to make way for so-called improvements.

England is rich in military and civil buildings: the castles of Windsor, Warwick, Kenilworth,

Rochester, and the Tower of London, are all well known and have been frequently described. Perhaps the most interesting of English civil structures of the Middle Ages, are the colleges at Oxford; as, however, they follow, in the Gothic treatment, the progress of the styles, as illustrated in the contemporary ecclesiastical edifices, they do not require special description.

The town-halls of Belgium are important Gothic buildings, and are found in all the principal cities of that country. Their flat façades are singularly rich, but as they embody only the forms and ornament of Gothic art, they are less interesting and poorer examples than any less pretentious structures showing the constructive element, which predominated in the Gothic style.

Toward the close of the style, and before the rebirth of Classic art had completely superseded Gothic architecture, a curious transitional style had a brief sway, in which both were blended. The wing of the Chateau de Blois, built by Louis XII., and the Chateau de Gaillon, built by Cardinal Amboise, in the year 1500, the façade of which is now preserved in the courtyard of the Ecole des Beaux Arts, may be regarded as the best specimens of this charming and short-lived art. The churches of St. Etienne du Mont, and St. Eustache, at Paris, may be added to these as typical of the contemporary religious edifices.

In them we see the last throes of a dying style

which had become extravagant and distorted in its final efforts to survive, but retained traces of its former beauty even in its expiring moments.

The Gothic style arose in the latter half of the twelfth century, it attained its greatest purity and simplicity in the thirteenth; during the fourteenth a more extensive use of ornament was introduced, in consequence of which it has been termed Decorated Gothic; finally, in the fifteenth, its principles and principal features were exaggerated and pushed to their utmost limits, until its brilliancy, flickering in the flamboyant traceries of the latest period, expired and gave place to a Classic revival.

XI.

THE RENAISSANCE.

A NOT uncommon error is made in applying the name Renaissance only to the delicately treated style of revived Classic art, such as was prevalent in France during the reigns of Francis the First, and his immediate successors.

The word—derived from the verb *renaître*, signifying in French the rebirth (of the classics understood)—cannot, however, be confined to any such narrowed limits, for no new style having been substituted since, it is as correct a term to-day as it was in the sixteenth century. There is certainly a distinction between the first brilliant productions of the revival, and the more ponderous buildings which succeeded them, but Early and Late Renaissance express this satisfactorily. It did not always follow, however, that all the work which, from its characteristics, would be classified under the first head, necessarily antedated that belonging to the later period.

In Italy, where the works of the Romans were too colossal to be utterly destroyed, and too conspicuous to be easily forgotten, the first movement naturally took place to reawaken the long dormant art, by which they had been produced.

In the fifteenth century Orcagna built the Loggia dei Lanzi, in Florence, and boldly substituted round arches for the pointed ones then in vogue. This was the turning-point in the tide of Gothic architecture, for it needed but little more to induce the delighted Italians to throw off the yoke of an art which they had adopted but unwillingly, and which had never been sympathetic to their taste. Consistently with their impetuous nature, the change was effected without hesitation in a marvellously short period, and with scarcely any of the usual intervening transitional stages. The ancient forms reappeared and replaced the dying Gothic as rapidly as in the days of the French monarchy the cry "Le roi est mort. Vive le roi!" heralded at once the king's death and his son's succession to power.

It is strange that there should have been so little to connect the succeeding styles, that the revival should have been so completely independent of and uninfluenced by a style which had been steadily growing for four centuries, and which men must have become accustomed to consider the only one suited to their times. Delicate workmanship was, however, the only Gothic legacy the Renaissance architects accepted, and this was the chief characteristic of the work of the early period. The proportions and scale of their buildings were small; a whole order: pedestal, column, and entablature generally occupying and marking the height of an ordinary story of fifteen or twenty feet, and the ornament used, while profuse, was executed in the lowest relief and with most minute detail.

If the revolution in art was great, it had proportionately great exponents: Brunelleschi, Bramante, Raphael, Sangallo, Vignola, Michael Angelo are names as prominent in history as those of much-lauded victors in the battlefield.

Brunelleschi, architect of the dome of St. Mary's in Florence, was one of the earliest innovators. He designed the Strozzi and Pitti Palaces in that city, with the horizontal lines and round arches of the Classic school, although still retaining the feudal traditions in their massive stone-work and in the austerity of their exteriors. The great palaces of Rome which belong to this period partake also of this external severity, and confine their brilliancy to interior display. The palaces of the Cancelleria by Bramante, the Palazzo Massini by Balthasar Perruzzi, of Sienna, the Sacchetti and Corsini Palaces by Sangallo, the Barberini designed by Bernini, and the Farnese Palace upon which Sangallo, Vignola, and Michael Angelo devoted their labors in turn, are a few among the most celebrated.

Most of these buildings, while varying in size and in accordance with the character of their sites, are rectangular in plan, and enclose quadrangular courts, the different stories being marked by superposed orders and arcades. They are planned on a liberal scale, with broad proportions and with great deference to symmetry. The beauty of the plan was, in fact, one of the best features of the new style, not only in domestic, but in ecclesiastical architecture, for the arbitrary Gothic arrangements being once discarded, it became possible to combine the circle and straight line in many novel and beautiful ways, for which the older Roman buildings furnished admirable examples. The study of these plans forms one of the most important elements in an architect's education, and their examination in these days of iron props and twelve-inch walls is fraught with much pleasure and profit.

The light and brilliant creations of the early period are abundant in Northern Italy, and were models with which the French were readily impressed. The façade of the church in the Certosa of Pavia, with its elaborate detail and delicate ornament, and such buildings as the Spinelli Rezzonico and Vendramin palaces, the church of St. Zachariah, the Logetta and Library of St. Mark's of Sansovino, in Venice, and farther South the Palazzo Fava in Bologna, the Capella Pazzi attached to the older Sta. Croce in Florence, and the monument to Julius II. in Sta. Maria del Popolo in Rome are a few beautiful examples of the early treatment which has so much affinity with the works produced in France under the Valois.

The great Italian cathedral upon which nearly all

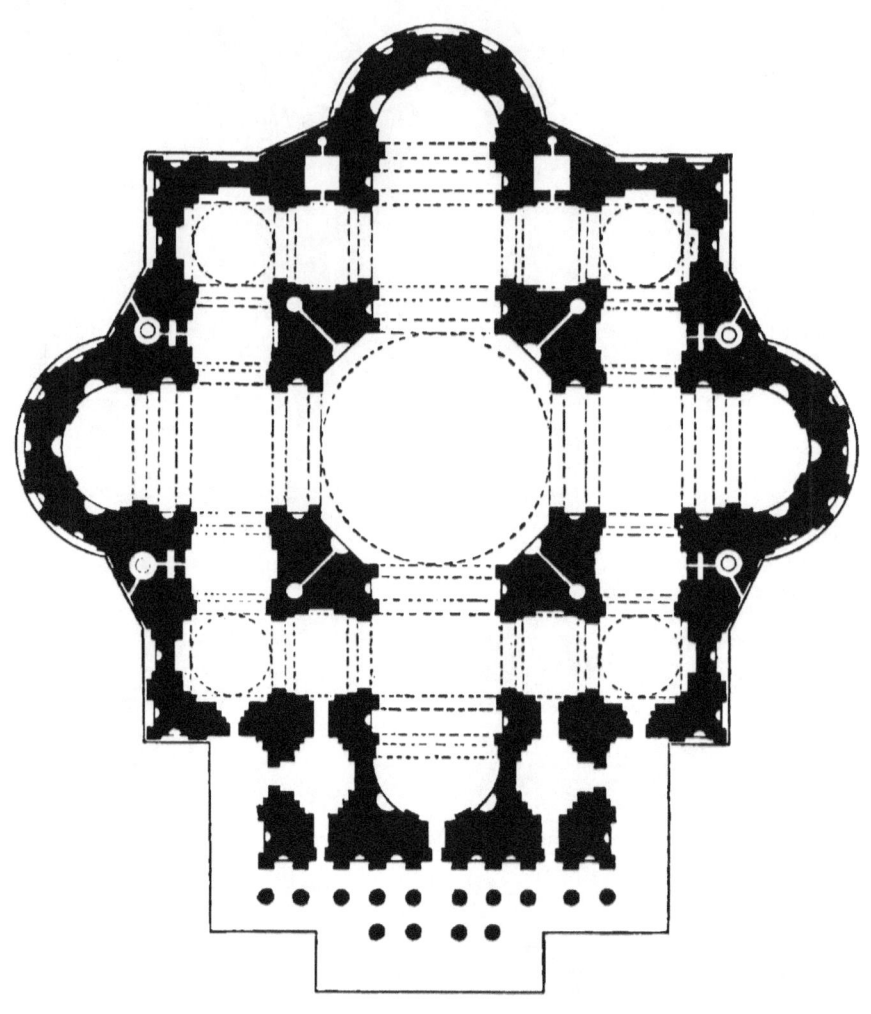

PLAN OF ST. PETER'S AS ORIGINALLY DESIGNED BY MICHAEL ANGELO.

subsequent churches were modelled was commenced upon the site of the old basilica of St. Peter's in Rome in the year 1506, upon plans by Bramante, and occupied a century and a half in completion. After Bramante, Giocondo, Julian Sangallo, Raphael, Peruzzi, Antonio di Sangallo, Michael Angelo and Carlo Maderno each worked upon it in turn.

Michael Angelo, who designed the dome, wished to adopt the plan of the Greek cross, that is, with equal arms, as shown in the accompanying plan. The result would have been much more monumental and would have given the dome its due effect within a moderate distance, while now it can only be properly judged from afar, and the high façade terminating the nave is both poor in composition and detrimental to the general conception. The building is essentially Classic in all its details, but differs from the general design of any particular Classical building. The nave is formed by a Corinthian arcade similar to those of ancient Rome, though on a vastly larger scale, supporting a tunnel-vault, which is decorated with sunken panels like those of the ancient Baths. The dome is supported on a circular drum carried on four immense piers and improves on the Pantheon only in size, while it is surpassed by St. Sophia in scientific construction.

The cathedral is most richly, even gaudily, decorated within, with coloured marbles and mosaics and contains numerous tombs of great magnificence and an altar with twisted columns designed by

Bernini. It is the largest church in the world, and yet its proportions are so harmoniously, or inharmoniously designed, that it does not produce a corresponding sense of its vastness upon the beholder. The single order occupying the height of two stories is a feature, the invention, or rather arrangement of which, is attributed to Michael Angelo. In subsequent buildings it was nearly always adopted in preference to the smaller orders marking each floor.

The life of this great artist forms of itself a chapter in the history of architecture. Michael Buonarotti, surnamed Angelo, the most brilliant architect of the sixteenth century, was born of noble parentage in Arezzo in the year 1575. He developed extraordinary talents at an early age, and after outstripping his first instructor, took up his residence in Florence, where he studied anatomy and the human figure until he became the most expert draughtsman of his time. In Rome, where he was summoned by Julius II., he produced several fine works in statuary, but owing to the jealousy of Bramante was forced to quit the city and return to Florence. There he aided the citizens to sustain a siege during a year, by his superior knowledge of fortification, and subsequently went to Venice, where he designed the famous Rialto bridge. At the earnest solicitation of the pope he returned to Rome and commenced the great paintings in the Sistine Chapel, to which work he had been assigned by the counsels of Bramante, who wished to prove his inferiority to his own nephew Raphael. The result of the work, completed in a marvellously short period, however, was so successful that all Rome ran to see it.

After the accession of Paul III. to the Papal see, Michael Angelo was definitely appointed architect of St. Peter's and worked on the building during the remainder of his life, although he returned to Florence several times and there executed the splendid statues which adorn the chapel of the Medicis. In his later days he was assisted by Vignola in his work, but died before its completion at the advanced age of eighty-eight.

Giacomo Barrozio, called Vignola from his birthplace near Bologna, is known for his great works, the chief of which are the Jesuits' church in Rome and the castle of Caprarolla at Viterbo, which he built for the Cardinal Alexander Farnese, and also, especially to architects, for the rules and measurements of Classical orders which he composed from the buildings of Rome with the aid of the manual of Vitruvius.

This work comprises the elements of design used in nearly all the buildings erected during the two following centuries, many of their elevations being simple combinations of different pages of Vignola's book, which to this day is the best guide for Classical proportions and the architects' A B C.

The discriminator between the various architectural styles is fond of drawing a marked distinction between Italian, French, and German Renaissance, and illustrating it by views of the typical Italian palace, with a flat tile roof and low pediments, and the typical French house, with immensely high slate roofs and pretentious dormers. Although the eye of the practised architect can distinguish between the representative work of Sansovino and Philibert Delorme, and between that of Bernini and Claude Perrault, yet such distinctions do not form separate styles, for they are but unimportant differences, caused by local influences.

The subject should be looked upon in a broader sense, for all these subdivisions tend to confuse the student and lead him to forget the sequence of the great historical style of which they form part.

The Jacobean, Queen Anne, and kindred so-called styles in England were merely eccentric streams flowing out of the one main channel, which were scarcely worthy of distinction and certainly not of revival in our times.

In France, under each reign, there was a slight difference of treatment, chiefly in the decoration of interiors, which permits of a classification most convenient to the modern upholsterer, but for our purposes it is sufficient to apply the two divisions—Early and Late Renaissance.

The Chateaux of Blois, Chambord, and Chenonceaux in the Valley of the Loire, the Palaces of Fontainebleau, St. Germain en Laye, the Tuileries and the old Louvre in Paris are splendid examples of the former, and monuments worthy of the great artists, Pierre Lescot, Philibert Delorme, Jean Goujon, and others, who laboured upon them. They are illustrative of the employment of the small orders and ornament in low relief, which characterized the corresponding period in Italy, though they are generally richer and more spirited in design than the Italian buildings, and the soft stone which is so abundant in France permitted more lavish ornament upon the exteriors.

The skeletons of each design, that is to say, the main architectural lines, stripped of elaborate detail, are much alike and can nearly all be brought back to the ancient method of superposing orders. This is no disparagement on the value of the work, for the plans of many buildings were excellent, and the variety of ornamental design was of a delicacy and imaginative beauty which has rarely been surpassed.

It is questionable, indeed, whether the change which took place in the century of Louis XIV., in the introduction of larger proportions and greater severity of ornament, was so much a gain as it was considered at the time. To this period belong some of the great churches modelled upon or rather suggested by St. Peter's in Rome: St. Paul's in London, rebuilt by Christopher Wren; the Val de Grace, the joint work of Lemercier, Leduc, and Mansart, and the church of the Hotel des Invalides in Paris, also by Mansart, are among the finest of the period and style.

The plan of the last-named church is appended as a particularly happy example in general arrangement and symmetrical variety, doing great credit to Mansart, who also built the larger portion of the celebrated Chateau de Versailles.

The publication of Stewart and Revetts' great work upon the antiquities of Athens called general attention in England to the beauty of Greek art, toward the close of the last century, and resulted in the erection of a number of buildings in imitation of Athenian monuments which were utterly inappropriate and unsuited to the English climate.

In France architecture went through two or three fashionable phases, from great extravagance of design under Louis XV. to extreme simplicity under Louis XVI., finally relapsing under Napoleon into the servile copying of entire Classic buildings: a great falling off from the principle of the sixteenth century work, which had always been original in conception although borrowing detail from the antique.

During the early part of this century, architecture sank to the lowest ebb all over the world, probably owing to the disturbing influences of the great Napoleonic wars. Within the last thirty years the spirited writings of a few enthusiasts and the liberal teachings of the French schools have caused a general revival, and better work is being done now than at any time during the century.

Avaricious commerce and the predominance of

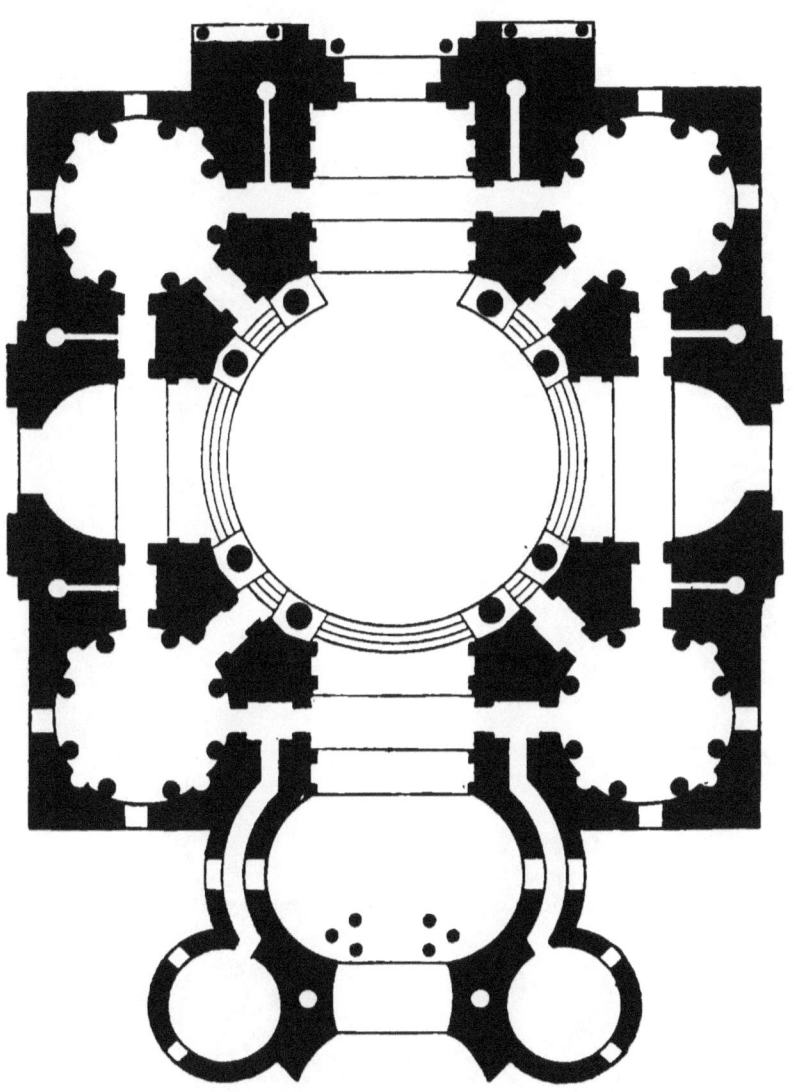

PLAN OF CHURCH OF THE HOTEL DES INVALIDES AT PARIS.

the desire for display rather than quiet love of the arts are factors which stand much in the way of genuine progress, but it is not improbable that the spread of refined education will eventually succeed in planting the seeds of this love in the heart of the great masses, and enable architecture to resume its natural and elevating position in their midst.

XII.

CONCLUSION.

AT the present stage of modern art we have the principles, broadly speaking, of two great styles of architecture to guide us in the design of the buildings which we may have to erect. These are the Classic and the Gothic; for we may apply the term Classic not merely to the works of the Greeks and Romans, but to their offshoots the Byzantine and Romanesque styles, the one branching Eastward and the other Westward, altered in many respects, but founded on the older systems; and we have seen that the Renaissance was but a revival of the same methods and forms.

In each of these styles the best result has always been attained where the constructional element has been held to be as important as the decorative, where the essential and useful have not been subservient to considerations of ornament or display. In Classic work much has been done that is unworthy, in the senseless repetition of columns and pilasters which support nothing, in decoration which serves only to conceal ill-adjusted architectural lines; and the same is equally true of degenerate Gothic, in which whole walls have been covered with meaningless panels, and massive buttresses built up to receive no strain.

Nevertheless, by following only what is good in the principles of each, and by avoiding the errors which experience has enabled us to perceive, especially those which have engrafted themselves upon us by bigoted custom, we can not only produce fine work but assist in the advance of architecture.

Before deciding upon what style to employ in the composition of an edifice, it is well to first consider thoroughly the programme of what is wanted in its plan, and then the special character with which we desire to invest it both exteriorly and interiorly. It is scarcely necessary to add that both should be intimately connected.

We have seen that the best period of Gothic art was that wherein the whole structure was raised on a theory of weights and strains thrown from vault to pier, and pier to buttress; it is, therefore, absurd, when a building occupies a space between the party-walls of modern street lots, to attempt an interior construction having the appearance of corresponding with buttresses and similar contrivances for which there is no room on the outside.

If, therefore, we choose Gothic for our style, let us follow no false theory, but work on the principles demonstrated in its innumerable examples, in which it may be possible to find room for further development, introducing no feature of construction which has not a full and consistent meaning.

One can scarcely go the lengths to which many venture, in saying that Gothic architecture is suited only to ecclesiastical buildings, for there are many splendid military and civil structures, from the keeps and castles of England and France, to the town-halls of Belgium. But there is this much to be said in their favour, that while the laws of fortification and domestic life have altered entirely since the Middle Ages, on the one hand, those governing the observances of religion have remained unchanged and no manner of building is so essentially religious in its character or better calculated to command the reverence and awe of the devotee, on the other.

In support of this view many will agree in admitting that there is nothing of this religious sentiment expressed in the Corinthian colonnades of St. Peter's, or, in fact, in any of the great number of Renaissance churches which are scattered throughout the cities of Europe, while it never fails to exercise its influence upon anyone entering the great Gothic cathedrals.

The great prevailing thought of Mediæval times was a religious one, and we see it reflected in the minutest details of the lives of the people of that age; it was, consequently, but natural that it should attain its highest expression when they filled their churches with the best that could be produced in architecture, sculpture, and painting.

While the Classic orders seem out of place in a temple of Christian worship they are appropriate in civil buildings, and we have no better examples for beauty of proportion. They are the result of the thought and taste of generations of architects and have stood the test of time, for they are as pleasing to-day as in the days of ancient Greece and Rome.

It is their proportion rather than their component parts which we should follow, for a column, unless needed as a support, is a questionable decoration, and pilasters or engaged columns are only desirable where additional thickness of wall is required, used as the Gothic architect would have used buttresses, and never as mere ornaments, which are at once a fraudulent delusion and a retrogression in the progress of architecture.

A multiplicity of columns and entablatures does not make perfect architecture, but great leading lines, good proportion, clear detail, and appropriate ornament.

The guiding rule is to do nothing which has not intrinsic merit. It is better to have an absolutely plain wall than one covered with poor decoration; far better to have no cornice at all than a galvanized iron one, painted to look like stone.

The true definition of architecture is "ornamental construction." It is not a utilitarian science, because if so there would be no *raison d'être* for beauty of design, for mere shelter and commodious arrangement could as well be provided by the engineer as by the architect. The art of the architect lies in the composition of buildings at once suited to their purpose and beautiful to the eye; and as such his art is one that can progress, not through a series of changing fashions which grow wearisome before they have lasted a decade, but step by step, according to the example of the great periods of the past.

This example teaches us never to copy slavishly, but to imitate old examples only so far as they may suit modern needs, in principle rather than in detail, and to eschew the reproduction of defects, however picturesque, so that architecture may be a living art instead of the mummified representation of archæological researches.

In pursuing the study of so vast and splendid an art we should do so with some feeling of reverence for its dignity, not looking upon it as a mere money-making trade, for the greatest architects the world has known have been satisfied in being only worshippers at a great shrine. Reverence is a sentiment slightly regarded in an age when delicacy of feeling in such matters is often held up as a butt for the jests and derision of the vulgar, and the dignity of the art has little foothold when it has become a custom for the vendor of cheap furniture to style his shop an "Art Repository," and the founder of cast-iron abortions to call his factory "The Art Metal Works."

Nevertheless all of our work must reflect something of our inner thoughts, and if we do not place them upon a high plane it is not possible for their reflection to contain what is noble and true. We cannot become artists in the true sense of the word without loving and reverencing the beauty and principles which have made the art so great a one.

It is the custom among certain people to sneer at sentiment, and call for practical art; but the most practical art is essentially the product of thoughtful sentiments.

As an illustration, let us compare the Laocoön, of sculpture; the Halls of Karnak, of architecture; the Dead March, of music; the " Descent from the Cross," of painting, with the " Dancing Faun," the arabesques of the Renaissance, the waltzes of Chopin, and the gay feasts depicted by Paolo Veronese, and the contrast shows us that each branch of an universal art expresses the opposite feelings of gravity or tragedy, of joy or comedy, each in its separate manner.

In designing, questions arise every moment which can only be decided by an innate sentiment of what is good and appropriate. There are no fixed laws governing the height of a spire or the projection of a moulding; they are matters which depend upon correct feeling, or, in other words, upon educated taste.

If it were not so, art would become a mechanical science, and could no longer be called by that name. Emotion has no place in mechanics, but it has great influence in the arts. We know the Greeks were an emotional race, and it is said that Michael Angelo wept before a beautiful statue or painting; and the works of the people and of the individual were proportionate to the depth of their feelings, and have perhaps never been excelled.

Let us, therefore, commence this study—for the omega of this book is but the alpha of architecture—despising none of its delicate subtleties, and endeavour to grasp its principles, in the hope of doing our share in its further advance, laying aside the petty gratification of our vanity in a genuine affection for our art.

THE END.

www.ingramcontent.com/pod-product-compliance
Lightning Source LLC
Chambersburg PA
CBHW022012220426
43663CB00007B/1058